CONVERSATIONS
with
JESUS

CONVERSATIONS
with
JESUS

An Intimate Journey

ALEXIS ELDRIDGE

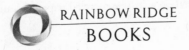

RAINBOW RIDGE
BOOKS

Cover and interior design by Frame 25 Productions
Cover photograph © Supri Suharjoto c/o Shutterstock.com

Published by:
Rainbow Ridge Books, LLC
140 Rainbow Ridge Road
Faber, Virginia 22938
434-361-1723

If you are unable to order this book from your local
bookseller, you may order directly from the distributor.

Square One Publishers, Inc.
115 Herricks Road
Garden City Park, NY 11040
Phone: (516) 535-2010
Fax: (516) 535-2014
Toll-free: 877-900-BOOK

Visit the author at:
www.alexiseldridge.com , www.conversationswithjesus.com
or www.loveisaverbarts.com

Library of Congress Cataloging-in-Publication Data applied for.

ISBN 978-0-9844955-1-1

10 9 8 7 6 5 4 3 2 1

Printed on acid-free recycled paper in Canada

Editor's Note

I remember years ago Neale Donald Walsch appeared on *Larry King Live* to talk about his extraordinary series of books called *Conversations with God,* which by that time had been on the *New York Times* bestseller list for over 170 weeks. One of the first questions Larry asked, in a somewhat gruff tone of voice, was, "How do you know you're talking to God?" To everyone's surprise, Neale responded that he didn't know. Larry relaxed. Okay, he was probably thinking, this guy is not certifiable. Neale went on to point out that no one could really know the information he received was from God—only that was how the source of his information identified itself. He wasn't vested in proving anything. He only requested that when people read the book, they decide for themselves if the information was meaningful to them, and if the knowing of which would make a difference in their lives.

Having edited and published both books, I can say that the same principle should apply for *Conversations with Jesus.* Alexis Eldridge calls Jesus an intimate friend, and talks to him every day. He wanted to write this book with Alexis and convey some information that he thought would be beneficial for people to know. Alexis also knows that there is no way she can prove that Jesus dictated these words. She can only know that these words did not, could not, have come from her own mind, and that to the depths of her soul, she believes that they come from Jesus. The fact is, either you believe in life after death or you don't. If you do, then it makes sense that time is different in that realm and it may certainly be possible to communicate with anyone who lived in any "time" period on the earth.

Much of what you will read in this book will gently change the perception of who Jesus was and what his role was in the brief time he was on the earth as the man they called Yeshua ben Joseph. I believe this book has the real message that he came to communicate to all of us. Jesus said that one can know the nature of a thing by the fruit it bears. Thus, Alexis can only ask that the reader decide if what is written here makes sense to them and if the thoughts and ideas ring true in their heart. I know they do for me.

Robert S. Friedman
June, 2010

This book is dedicated to the Creators. For its content is intended to remind all the children of creation who they are meant to be, and are able to be, and to clearly know the support that abounds to help us.

Acknowledgments

I offer my deepest gratitude to Jesus for beckoning me to co-create this book with him. I also thank him for his trust in me.

Thanks to Bob Friedman, publisher, now friend, for knowing there were more conversations in need of hearing, and suggesting that I write them down. I also appreciate his encouraging words and the acknowledgment of my *knowing*.

Finally, to Kristine Sensenig, I send a bouquet of chocolate flowers for the heart that she put into this book while typing and editing.

Introduction by Jesus

My dear fellow sons and daughters of the Creators,

It's through this book made manifest that my own prayers have been answered. It was my dream to have someone, other than those who have already done so, speak on my behalf. And, it was also my dream that the sharing be done in a way that would not further confuse people who come to hear my teachings, stories of difficulties, and the ways I got through them.

Both Alexis' belief in her experiences of my time by her side, and her unadulterated quest and need for truth no matter what the cost or consequence, has offered me all I needed. She has allowed me to share the information with which you will soon be blessed. Before now, my heart longed to be heard. Out of exile, chains dangling, open and free, I welcome you to our conversations—which are completely directed toward what I know is the highest good.

Our conversations are meant for inspirational and transformational purposes. Both Alexis and I allowed only our truths to speak in the pages that follow. Our time together was organic. There was no planning of the topics that were addressed. We knew trusting in the divinity coming through us would be the right way to proceed.

Let it be known that there will be stories and information that you may not have heard before. I encourage you to allow yourself to remain open and to receive what is meant for you. Time continues to go by so quickly. Grasping for crumbs of harmony and joy is not what your life ought to be about. Be assured that it's definitely not the reason you're here.

My intention for everyone who travels the pages of this book is for them to find their way out from underneath the layers of falseness that make up much of modern society— so that the beauty of who they are, and of the course they are meant to be walking, will be clearly known. Through my real teachings, personal challenges, and joys, may my intention become reality.

Lovingly,

Jesus

Introduction by Alexis

How does a Jewish woman from Brooklyn become best friends with Jesus? I ask myself this still, even though it has been quite some time now. Although when I reflect upon it, there is some indication of the answer. I see myself as a young girl in the single digits. I'm at an adult gathering of my father's friends—standing in the background and watching them. It was at that time when I first knew there was something different about me—something different from the rest of my family. I asked my father to step out of the group, so that I could speak with him. I then told him I knew what everyone was feeling and thinking. He smiled strangely, went back to his friends, and we never spoke of it again.

Many additional occurrences in my youth continued to encourage me to suppress my intuition. It was painful then, living through my teens and twenties, having forgotten what I once knew . . . .

I first noticed Jesus about ten years ago. A symbol related to him appeared in a painting I had done. The difficult choice to not smear the form, so that it would become once again only color, changed my life in myriad ways—including recovering my intuition. He then became a presence in various poems. I began writing about his strife, and the way he loved. It was as if I knew him intimately. I felt him and his life's experiences.

I started believing that there was someone I could relate to—another who had been judged, misunderstood, and not appreciated for his way of being. I didn't question how I knew this, having never been exposed to a Bible or what he taught. It simply felt natural and right.

An actual relationship began a few years after the time I've just described. Through a guided visualization with a group of others, all being led to meet our individual spirit guide, he came to me. He let me know he was the one. It was surprising, despite what had come before. Previously it had been a bit of a mystery. This made it real. I understood, at that point, that the groundwork was being laid. Through the painting and the poems, he was becoming accessible to me as I was becoming open to him. And at the age of thirty-three, feeling ready for a new chapter of my life to begin, one with more richness and meaning, the most loving being I had ever known showed up to guide me there.

It took some time for me to accept him into my life on a regular basis. But I did. Learning how to hear him fully also took practice. The most significant challenge was believing in his guidance and trusting in my experience of it. I often wondered if it was just my vivid imagination creating it all. As his guidance began to prove itself to be that which was for the highest good (which was not something I was used to), my belief strengthened. My daily experiences became less threatening, more understandable, and I felt deeply supported. Life was unfolding as I was hearing it would.

All of this, and more, has led me here—writing the introduction to a book about what Jesus wants to be known. The book was first encouraged by a friend I had told that Jesus and I spoke together regularly. The idea came as a surprise. And yet, when I asked Jesus if that's what he wanted, I heard a clear confirmation. However, I didn't know if I could do what he asked. "How will I know which questions to ask you?" I said. "Will I be able to really hear your answers clearly enough to transcribe them?" I was then reminded of the pages and pages of written information I had received for myself, by hearing him. And yet, it was still inconceivable to be able to do it for others with such precision and deliberateness.

Before I agreed, I wanted to practice. I was afraid that I would fail, so I decided to be very nonchalant about it. One autumn day, driving around in my pickup a long way from Brooklyn, I asked Jesus the type of question to which I thought people would want to hear an answer. He answered me with vital information, and I heard it clearly. I was then one step closer to committing.

A few more weeks went by and then our process of written conversations began. Autumn was ending and the nights now had a chill to them. One in particular had a little more obvious magic that it wanted to share. I was pulling into a parking space at my local DVD rental shop, enjoying the last few lyrics of an unfamiliar folk song. What I heard, although I can't recall the exact words, I'm now going to share:

"We spend our lives learning ways to live . . .when really it's about learning how to live from the truth of who we are."

Those words sum up my life so far and why I agreed to co-create this book. Those words have also proven themselves to be the theme of what you are about to read. It is my deep wish that this sojourn leads you to the truth of who you are.

Through grace and with gratitude,

Alexis

CONVERSATIONS
with
JESUS

November 28, 2009

It's day one of Jesus and my conversations being recorded for ears other than mine. It's a first. With a blank spiral-bound notebook and a new black pen, I sit at my second-hand table and await his presence.

Jesus says:

> I'm going to start by thanking you for agreeing to work with me, so that I may share all I've been yearning to express. Dear one, you are always loyal to our friendship.
>
> I would like to proceed by you asking any questions you would like to have answered. I will also initiate conversations and topics I deem are in need of some light.
>
> Please begin.

I respond:

The first topic I'm curious about is happiness. Why are so

many people unhappy? Is one supposed to be happy at all times?
If so, how is this done?

> Ah . . . happiness. A long time ago, when people were
> not overly concerned with material items, they could sense
> that they were already whole. They were not controlled by
> fear and doubt. They had boldness when it came to know-
> ing their truth. This is no longer the case, due to society's
> belief that their great power is housed without—rather
> than within.
>
> This relates to the church's choice to continue telling
> people that I am their only savior. This depletes their own
> sense of power, resulting in a continued intangibility of the
> overall happiness they could have. I am not a savior in the
> assumed sense. You all have enormous power because of
> the divinity living inside you.
>
> It is this knowledge of your own personal power, and
> the direct experience of it, that leads to the truest sort of
> happiness.

Are you telling me that you're not God? I know most sects
of Christianity believe that you are.

> Despite what people believe, it's most important to
> have the truth be known. I am no more God than all of the
> people and the creatures you live amongst on a daily basis.
> Many theologians already know who I am; that I walked the
> earth in the flesh, and that what I did, others can also do.
>
> I had opportunities to dwell on my past pain, to not for-
> give, to feel punished, to believe myself to be victimized. I
> chose not to. Instead, all those human emotions were chal-

lenged and released. In their place arose other emotions; emotions that were more like those experienced by God.

I listened to God through the old scriptures and through my own relationship. We would speak together and, due to that, I learned how to live in the world without being consumed by human emotions. What I believed, then what I learned to live, and what I eventually taught is: love all that is alive, regardless of whether that love is merited or not.

God showed me how deep loving can go. As I returned from the desert, I was fed and nurtured without ever falling ill—just like I heard would happen. I didn't need to let human desires overshadow my divinely given personal power. However, I had to learn all of this in order to truly be able to teach it.

This describes a small part of my human life, and this is why some people believe me to be God—the one and only. I was God-like, as are you and your fellow humans. It is both my hope, and that of the Creators, that this will become clearer in the teachings on the following pages.

"Creators?" Are you saying there is more than one God?

Yes, "Creators" is most accurate. Dear one, "God" is a term more commonly used instead of "Creators." However you needn't believe it is a sufficient title for the male and female energies that have made everything possible by their merged forces. "God" is simply a term used to make it easier to discuss. God/Creator/Source/Divine Energy/Universal Truth . . . these, and others, are all words that could be used to describe all that has come before everything else. Despite all the familiar terms, it is unfamiliarity with the very essence of their meaning that makes the terms a distraction and keeps people from living through their own divinity.

Tell me how someone can learn to live as you described, as you did, when you were flesh.

Worry no longer what your neighbor will think of you; bring about the most truth you can, at any and all moments. This is the first way to align with source energy. Nothing other than the absolute truth ought to be expressed at all times, despite whatever excuses you may find for doing otherwise. When one doesn't always bring forth honesty, one's truest knowing of the divine—within and without—drifts farther and farther away.

I know, from my personal experience, that honesty isn't always appreciated. Often, I've been on the receiving end of lies and I've witnessed people lying to each other. How can this be changed in our present society, so that this plague can end?

It wasn't long ago that telling the truth was valued more highly. Corruption, however, has become accepted. America, as well as other powerful countries (at least by human standards), has diminished the value placed on integrity and authenticity . . . due to the hunger for the almighty dollar. Learning more about integrity—true integrity—and living by it with full commitment, would not only change your planet's epidemic, it would allow for the ceasing of environmental hazards that are not reversing quickly enough. For they, too, are a result of dishonesty.

Are you confirming global warming, and do you want to talk now about environmental concerns?

It appears as though my passion, having been caged for so long, is now coming through profusely—pardon my fury. The answer to your question is "yes." Your planet's birth was a sacred event. All that had to be done in order to value and honor its life-giving force was to not allow greed to play a leading role. However, greed does. And it has created an extreme imbalance.

Crises abound, despite the many efforts by environmental and amnesty organizations. And yet, it's not too late for a turnaround. But it needs to be fast. Within five to ten years, the planet's population will be more than it can handle. Precautions need to be taken now. The population needs to decrease. Please heed my words. Now is the time to stop reproducing at the current rate. Resources need to be replenished. It is time for a planetary rebirth.

This all sounds pretty scary. I don't want to be the bearer of bad news.

Dear one, you are only the messenger of what is already known but not being taken seriously enough. Hence, I need to share this through you. Shine some light: it's the only way to allow what's hidden in darkness to be seen.

What is something that people would find acceptable to do in order to help this situation?

[I hear and see Jesus laughing. I'm waiting for an answer.]

It ought not be about what is acceptable. That's no longer the current question. Rather, the question is: What is right for the good of all involved? This now needs to be the sole question, when determining one's next step with regard to the healing of the planet. It's a question that is also meant to be asked regularly, to determine how to live in alignment with one's purpose. With regard to one's answer, well that can be heard by truly listening to one's own heart.

Okay, now you know what I'm going to ask next. Thank you for the perfect lead, although I'm still reeling from the heaviness of the last topic. However, people are going to want to know: Do we, each of us, have a purpose?

Of course. So many humans, however, have not yet explored long enough to learn of it. When I walked the earth in human form, most people had little money. To a large degree, this kept them from having the time and opportunity to explore what excited them, moved them and illuminated them.

Now, large sums of money finds its way around more of the planet than ever before. However, fear of not being able to endure if one steps away from the flock (to my sadness) plays a significant role in preventing the most important experience there is: to become consciously in union again with the creative forces, by fully aligning with one's own creative force. This is what you call purpose.

What are you suggesting we do?

To begin, let it be taught from kindergarten through

high school that each person has a reason for being. That it's not about repeating what was done before. One's path could be similar to one that came before, but it ought to be undertaken in the individual's own way. Children need to know the truth about life—how it is meant to be a creative and loving time, supportive and encouraging of individuality.

There is not only the need for the divine plan to be known. It's the lack of knowledge of its presence that has been the rule; eliciting a pervasive sense of purposelessness.

November 29, 2009

⟨⟨⟨

Today I'd like some understanding regarding why there is so much sadness, rather than satisfaction, when all the people I meet appear to have as much as they could ever want or need?

The main reason people are sad has to do with not allowing themselves complete accessibility to the entire core of their being. It's the cutting off from the various parts of themselves that creates and maintains this sadness of which you speak.

You see, what you do not express will not disappear, however much you wish it to. But rather, in service to one's spirit, its hidden status will be illuminated by triggering that which is called "sadness." Sadness, therefore, is not the problem. Rather it's an arrow pointing to a dammed river inside oneself that is in need of flow.

November 30, 2009

A client of mine today asked me why I thought most "romantic" relationships don't last. This question came after I intuitively sensed that his enlarged prostate had to do with the sorrow with which he was quietly living. I mentioned it. He then shared he wished he had had a long-term, loving relationship rather than multiple marriages and brief relationships since.

I told him I thought my answer would be best put off so we could move forward with the healing treatment. I now will pose it to you.

Why don't "romantic relationships" last?

Ah . . . one of the biggest questions. And so it will remain, I'm sorry to say. Not because there aren't answers. Rather, due to the very nature of society's unwillingness to accept the answers.

The love between two people, however difficult this is to accept, is only supposed to last a certain length of time.

After that time, two people can still love one another but in a new way—remaining connected, but unattached. Love is an action. This is the way love is meant to be experienced.

"Romantic" love is not a problem. It's an attainment that requires releasing when the time is ripened.

Are you saying divorce is okay?

Your society's idea of marriage is what leads to divorce, not the coming together to love and be loved of which I am speaking.

Marriage: a union between beloveds, intoxicated by life's genuine light that shines from the galaxies through all of the Creators' living things. This kind of commitment between two people is destined to withstand the hills, valleys, fires, and floods and is meant to be harmonious for its appropriated time. Without this true understanding of life, no one will feel peace within and without—regardless of whether or not they're sharing it with another.

How does one acquire this understanding? It's not taught early in life—or late, for that matter. At least it wasn't taught to me. I'm just starting to develop deeper awareness, due to my experiences since I answered the call to be a healer.

So you say you "answered the call to be a healer." Alone? Certainly not! Did you not look toward spirit, in all of its many forms and guises? You were looking for more meaningful work and a more inclusive relationship with the partner you were with at the time. But, on a deep level, you didn't know how to make your life become the way you intuitively knew it ought to be. I am aware of this only because my spirit has known you—for your whole life.

And so dear one, I share all of this about you—not for any other reason than to illustrate that, despite the knowing you already had inside yourself, you offered it up as being your sole guide, in exchange for allowing the divinity all around you to have its role in guiding you as well.

So, it sounds as if you're saying intuitiveness is the way to understanding life. And by intuitiveness, I mean listening to one's body sensations, attending to natural organic ideas that come into one's head, and welcoming guidance from the universe. Hence, the way to engage harmoniously with another requires intuition. Living this way, with this direct understanding, should also allow two people to accept separation when the time comes.

You understand correctly! I want others to know how important it is to live by one's intuition. As you have illustrated in your journey, it leads one clearly on his or her path.

The thing is, so many people lose—or, more accurately, suppress—their intuition. Studying psychology taught me this. Working as a clinician with traumatized children showed it to me. And being in my own skin allowed me to know it.

As a child, I knew certain things to be true. When I brought this to an adult's—or even another child's—attention, so often the person would deny their role in the event or circumstance in question.

After a while, I began to not trust myself and my "knowing." Eventually, I was able to recover being able to know—believing it and calling it intuition. But it has been a long road!

It's not only the lies of others that leads one to doubt, feel shame, and stray from one's own knowing, as you experienced as a child. It's also fear of doing what "ought" not be done. It is the desire to not be shunned by others. So there is a concern about their opinions. Ironically, it is usually the opinion of those who are not stepping into their own views fully; who are not actualizing.

Quite often, this fear of allowing what we know to be true to come forth is related to the fear of shining brighter than another. However, not allowing our own light to shine (which is the outcome of living intuitively) can create a false sense of comradery and fulfillment. Therefore, not allowing one's light to shine promotes a belief system that is based on not believing, or listening to, one's intuition.

When you walked the earth in Israel, you exemplified hearing your own truth and trusting it enough to live by it—and die by it. Your truth was that you heard the Creators speak to you and guide you. You trusted your own intuition to not place doubt on your experience. And this fear you speak about—the fear of shining brighter than another—you didn't give into it. You shone your brightest. And you taught that everyone ought to do likewise. That it is our role.

This insight inspires another important subject: differences. Why is society, at large, unable to accept each others' differences in opinion, politics, philosophy, and so on?

It's more than differences in actions and thoughts being unaccepted; it's about the people themselves feeling unaccepted. Many of your society's problems have to do with this. Racism, sexism, ageism all have to do with the lack of acceptance of the individuals. Believing one person is less than another person is where problems start. So it is where I will start my answer to your question.

America's newest president, a man who is not always accepted solely because of his color, shows the pervasiveness of the challenge society needs to overcome. So you see, differences not being accepted can only really be resolved after the core issue is cleared.

Racism, ageism, and sexism all come from a single belief that one is not good enough! This belief is supported by make-up companies, "beauty" product producers, clothing designers and so on. They compound what has already been infused into modern society's infrastructure. With every new perfume, hair dye, de-wrinkle cream, facial moisturizer (in addition to actors signing on to promote the need for all these improvement-makers), more and more people are encouraged to look and feel unlike who they truly are!

Although the belief that one is not good enough as-is gets supported by all of this, the core belief comes only from the not-knowing—from failing to recognize that we are all the sons and daughters of divine creation; the Creators. And, therefore, we are perfect—already.

December 1, 2009

Now that you've shared what keeps us from knowing the truth about ourselves, how can one begin to live from this state of awareness?

> It wasn't that long ago that you didn't realize you were divine Light. You allowed others' voices to say what you ought to have said—and you agreed with what was not your truth. But you also surrendered Alexis—despite not knowing what, or who, would be there to support you. And also, you let go of that for which you once yearned—home, partnership, friends at any cost. And so I call on you to assist in answering your own question.

I'm a bit surprised at your request. I thought you would be teaching everything. Yet, I'm okay with it. I'm thirty-eight presently and, as I think back, it wasn't until age twenty that a wise older woman—the mother of the young man I was dating—introduced me to the idea of having a relationship with God. She told me that I could talk with God, and receive guidance and love.

She shared this notion with me in a way that offered no judgment. It changed my life. I began considering my actions and beliefs because I believed someone cared about them, and about me.

It wasn't long after this woman and I became friends that I left Arizona, where we had met, and moved back to New York. She and I stayed in contact. However, living in New York City got a hold of me for a while and I didn't speak with God as often. Distractions all around became enticing and predominant. I found myself suffering and also feeling a sense of emptiness; even though I was eating at my favorite restaurants, seeing shows, and shopping at luxury department stores.

It didn't take long before the pain became overwhelming. I had to make changes. I stopped dating the wrong guys, I gave up makeup and uncomfortable clothing, and I started noticing more of my inner workings.

I learned that I had a lot of fears. After enough discomfort from relating and not relating with myself and others, I began to work through them. I started looking deeper to understand what was happening, instead of accepting what wasn't feeling right.

This led me to counseling, and then to studying Buddhism. I felt at home engaging in the practices. I liked the idea that meditating in front of a statue of a Buddha meant I was connecting with my potential, not praying to something outside of myself.

Am I taking too long to answer the question?

I'm interested in all your sharing. Continue, for I know you're meaning to only illuminate the depths of how intense and long the journey was to recover the realization that you are light.

I appreciate your joy in my expression. I hope it will serve others, as they hear my story and reflect on their own lives.

Buddhism offered me a way to walk with integrity in the world. I hadn't learned that as a youth. Yet, I had trouble recalling the teachings when things got challenging. I still didn't trust myself, and I definitely didn't know who I really was.

It sounds as if you "knew" the changes you had made were assisting in your evolution. And still, clarity about who you are hadn't been revealed yet. Did this keep you engaging in painful distractions?

Yes. For a while. However, I was led to the next doorway and then the next. And through the willingness to enter, I've arrived here. I now have a clearer understanding of my divine nature than ever before.

Everyone's story is different—as are the reasons that lead one to, or away from, his or her realization of his or her true essence. However, each of you is truly a divine creation. You are divine energy. You are a creative force. And you can begin to live from this state of awareness by simply believing it is so.

Children need to hear this early on, in their youth—by living in an environment that cultivates their understanding via children's books, conversations with family members, in schools and through mass media. Synagogues and churches have to unite, treating all who enter a place of worship as light—as divine Creations who will one day be saints.

Let us encourage people to know that which lives inside them, so that more and more "saints" can be birthed. Let us educate them until they no longer hear who they are not and what they are lacking. Until they love themselves and one another, in light, like our Creators.

How can one move away from believing there is one God as their source of support, guidance, and "salvation," and come to understand that each person is a candle from the same flame?

This truth can become known through intimacy with one's challenges, and overcoming them by going through them. One can then know their wholeness where mind, body, and spirit are one.

Mind, body, and spirit only become divided when one believes it is so. And it is this division that supports the belief that one is not light, and that only I am . . . or that "God" is. However, with the realization that all three are part of one's divine energy, a completeness can be known. One becomes in tune with oneself and the division can, for once, be withered away.

Being in tune with oneself starts the relationship of trusting one's intuitive knowing. Hence, one begins to see and believe, through personal experience, that he or she is light.

To become in tune with oneself . . . would you share a way, or ways, for people to do this? It seems to be the basis for almost everything you've already explained.

In order for people to fully know who they are, they need to become in tune with themselves. All the physical sensations one knows to be specific to himself or herself are points of information for potential exploration. Nuances, such as a tickle in one's throat when talking about something, are intended to be monitored and understood. Another way of tuning into oneself has to do with sensing what is occurring in one's environment. For example: the ability to sense one's own feelings, as well those of others, lets one know with whom—or with what—one most resonates.

It is this resonance that also informs you of your character traits, likes, dislikes, and issues in need of resolution. It can also indicate where someone has evolved from, or the future direction in which he/she is evolving—like a mirror.

During my own earthbound experience, the ability of individuals to acquire true knowledge of their identity by tuning in to themselves—and/or the environment around them—was an unspoken concept. However, despite not hearing about it, some were doing it. I was one of them.

Much of the time that I spent alone, and with my family and friends, was an opportunity for me to gain insight into myself. These insights came from observing my own ways—as well as the ways of people, trees, mountains, flowers, and animals.

So, how did you actually do this observation?

Other than when I was teaching, I talked very little. Rather, I listened to the particular Spirit that wanted to talk with me, when I was alone. When I was in a desert or a forest, or by a river, I would watch the natural world and hear what it wanted to say to me. And when I was with another person, I would listen for a while—then I would encourage silence, so I could really hear them.

It was through all of this, dear one, that angels began to show me what I needed to know, in order to live life as I did—with clarity of who, and what, I was—without fear.

This I share so that people will be inspired to know themselves as deeply as possible—not only to fulfill their purpose, but also to fully know their power within. This knowledge will enable them to enjoy the journey.

To enjoy the journey. This is difficult for many people, including myself at times. Although the less I'm attached to how a situation is going to turn out, the more I enjoy it. This also helps me see how everything is connected. It helps me witness and experience the tapestry of life.

You say it's difficult for you to enjoy the journey "at times." So when is it not difficult? What are the conditions that allow for your enjoyment, other than not being attached to an outcome?

Well, interestingly enough, it goes back to what you were teaching earlier—observing self, other, and the environment. I learned to do this from my spirit guides as a way to know if what I'm feeling, or thinking, is my own or something I'm sensing in my environment. When I do this, I definitely enjoy the journey more.

Often, in the past, I would start feeling some strong emotion that would make that moment feel challenging. For a while, I thought I was each of the things I felt. For example, I would suddenly start feeling depressed. So, I would think about my circumstances and decide I had reasons for feeling as I did. This would make me hold onto it, subconsciously. I wanted it to be gone, and yet I identified with it. At that point, it would gravely affect my life.

Since I began my work as an energy healer, I have a clearer understanding that we take on energy that isn't ours. I combined this concept with what the spirit world has taught me about observing what is going on inside myself and around me, without judgment. Through this, I'm able to distinguish what is mine and to let go of what is not mine. This truly is helping me enjoy the journey more.

> I know people don't want to "take on" other people's energy. Allowing the danger of this to be known, as you have, provides much needed awareness. Would you offer any additional information to further clarify this issue?

Everything, in my understanding, is made up of energy: thoughts, people, houses, land, etc. Therefore, the energy from any circumstances has the potential to stay with us.

With this awareness, and the use of one's intention, I believe the shift could be made in regard to staying in one's own energy. Intention, as I've learned through experience, is powerful.

> Please share more about this! But before you do, it's important that you know that the way you work as a healer is also how I offer healing when you need it.

I sensed it was the same. However, I hesitate to talk about such personal intimacy. I must admit when you shared with me initially that you wanted to have your messages known, and asked me if I would do this dialogue project with you, I thought it would be primarily about you!

Your life, dear one, is now, and has been for quite some time, focused on healing. Once you honored the calling to commit to going without certain comforts and normalcies, you attained your purpose. This very much has to do with me—and also with you. So please do not hesitate. For through your story, I'm seeing the birthing of more and more pairs of wings on your earth-bound brothers and sisters.

Wow. It's still at times hard for me to fully realize where I've landed, here with you. So I'll honor your request, and share a bit more about foreign energy. It collects like dust in an empty room. I mean, it simply happens. We take on energy from our parents, siblings, teachers, lovers, children, and strangers. All the while, our own becomes harder to know because it gets covered up and scattered. The great news is that our own energy can be restored when the foreign energy is released. This is the healing work I do with others. The healing is actually of one's spirit becoming whole again. To me, it is truly a remarkable way to work with the nature of things.

December 7, 2009

You have definitely captured what I want others to know. Healing is not about fixing anything. Rather, it's about re-aligning one's spirit with his or her purpose. Often, when a person doesn't feel well or has a diagnosed illness, it's worth exploring deeply how illuminating this dis-ease can be in a person's life. It therefore assists him or her in becoming more aligned with his or her essence.

However, I don't want you to believe this is everyone's situation. Sometimes, despite the person's understanding, it may be time for him or her to leave the earth for a while. They may have completed their purpose. However, there are many who live daily without awareness of all they are meant to be doing. These people, if affected by illness, are being offered a contingency. Awakening to their purpose will allow both a pardon from an unhappy life (whether it is outwardly spoken or not) and from dis-ease, which in these cases, is a lack of alignment and an imbalance with their spirit.

This inspires my curiosity about having children—meaning, to have them or not. Many folks I've met say they don't have time to consider their purpose because they're spending all their time parenting. Would you comment on this?

Having another being to teach, care for and love—for some, this is their purpose. But know that this is only for some. There are many people who are avoiding their purpose by becoming parents. These people instead watch their child find theirs. They do this because they've adopted the belief system of someone else. This, in turn, causes despair, which is then often handed down to the child. This child will know intuitively that its life really doesn't belong to it. Rather, it's the unlived life of the parents. Hence, creating another unhappy being on the planet. And you already know the effect that causes.

Unfortunately, this happens quite often. There are many unhappy people, due to this way of living. Sadness permeates the spirit of a human who is not allowing his or her own purpose to be known—both to him or herself and to the world.

Besides following a belief system other than one's own, why else do people do what you're describing, and put off their own lives by bringing another into the world?

In part, the reason is that they don't know they have their own purpose outside of making another human. Distracting oneself, so as to not allow oneself time to simply exist, keeps one not knowing. Let it be known, however, that fear is the most significant cause. This fear would be eradicated by greater awareness of the richness of every human spirit's well of creativity.

People are not taught to know the depth of their creativity, and this leads to not knowing one's purpose. As you've seen , from working in New York City schools for as long as you did, most schools will cut creative education to a minimum when facing financial challenges—such as art, music, drama, and movement. In some cases, they are extinguished and justified by budget constraints. Clearly, the opportunity to truly know oneself as a creative force is then challenged. This is related to the fear of which I speak.

The scared humans who make these decisions truly believe one god created the world. And that they ought not compare themselves, or consider having also, this creative ability. They fear punishment and consequences if they don't abide by the antiquated, yet generally endorsed, doctrine. In actuality, these individuals are indeed trying to negotiate how all people are supposed to be living.

When one has no idea who (and what) they are, they cannot recognize truth on the deepest level. They can still feel safe paddling in the shallow water. Yet, I'm encouraging everyone to explore the deeper water—where they can no longer feel the ground.

What you're saying is quite deep in itself. It makes me want to take a break and digest it. However, the pages won't write themselves so . . . many people are not happy in their romantic partnerships. What can you let us know about why this is?

It was Mary Magdalene who taught me how to relate romantically. After she gave up the lifestyle she was living when we first met, we became loving friends and

confidants. Her energy was such that I was quite tempted
to engage in a lover's relationship with her. However, despite our mutual attraction and love, we did not.

True happiness in relationships comes from remaining real in each other's presence and when all actions
between the two parties are for the highest good—and for
that alone. I chose to not get physically intimate because
I wanted to shield her from pain. It wasn't that I wouldn't
have been able to walk away when so called. Her heart was
a bit more fragile than mine, and would not have healed as
quickly—from needing to let me go.

All intimate relating requires clarity about boundaries
and abilities. This is true on the emotional, spiritual, and
physical levels. (I speak of these divisions of intimacy to
encourage greater understanding, and because I know it's
the terminology with which you're familiar.) Integrity also
ought to play a large role in this. This means speaking and
living by one's own truth, while also knowing the other's
truth well enough to not disregard it. True companionship
cannot be had by only considering one's own wellness.

I feel deep sadness at how unknown so many couples
are to each other. Sex has become the ground on which
relationships are often being built. I declare, with full knowing, that sex ought to be the planted garden only after the
debris has been cleared and stones for a home have been
gathered. It is one stone among many, to be set carefully
with earth to hold them together.

You speak so poetically about couple-hood. I'm sure people
will want specifics about loving . . . in this way.

I'm encouraged by the way you have been relating in

your own "romantic relationships" for two-plus years now.
Would you be willing to share how you have acted?

Again, an unexpected return of the question. And yet, I do
believe I have evolved in this area to a degree worthy of sharing—a bit. One of the most significant experiences did occur
just over two years ago. I had been without a lover/companion
for some time and was feeling the absence. And, as the universe
always provides, I met an attractive, funny, and spiritually-ori-
ented guy—who shared my age and my same small town. This
was rare; meeting someone who had all these criteria and with
whom I could also share enjoyable conversation.

I found out early on that he smoked marijuana regularly,
but wanted to "quit." The man before him drank alcohol regularly, and also wanted to "quit"—or, as he said, "stop." That was
a difficult year of my life.

Here I was, now being confronted with a new person with
whom I had much more in common. Yet, I decided to not have
a relationship with him—except for a casual friendship. This
was very hard for me to do.

I chose to love myself more than I had before. I knew in
the core of my being that, although some qualities in this man
matched what I knew I required in a partner, some did not. And
these were non-negotiable. I also chose to love him fairly and
honestly by not agreeing to his offer to not smoke on days he
planned to see me. I chose to not ask him to change. Rather, I
shared clear information about my boundaries and about what
I needed. I saw, despite initially not wanting to do so, that it
was not an opportunity for either one of us to engage in a deep
union.

This led to a strengthening in myself, and greater clarity
about who I was—and am. It taught me to be more patient
about allowing time for the universe to deliver the right mate. I

do, at times, long for a sacred connection. I also know that, for it to be truly sacred, I need to be right for the man who comes into my life—and he for me. And, I mean "right" in ways that didn't matter, or even occur, to me some time ago—when it was more about instant pleasure or momentary comfort.

December 9, 2009

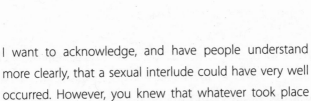

I want to acknowledge, and have people understand more clearly, that a sexual interlude could have very well occurred. However, you knew that whatever took place with this man would not support what you were (and are) calling forth in your life. In other words, you were not allowing anyone into your life who was clearly unable to care for himself. You knew that a relationship with such a person could not come forth purely—without resentment, anger, and other detriments to your own self-care.

In order to find true love, as opposed to brief sexual encounters, it is essential that one know oneself. Those who enter relationships without understanding their own idiosyncrasies, triggers, and availability (for emotional, physical, sexual, and other experiences) are signing up for pain.

I'm encouraging self-awareness—to the degree that a fire of emotionality can be prevented and divine timing can be allowed, so that experiences and people may appear as destined.

How about if we now discuss making love versus casual sex. I often hear people use the term "making love" when really they mean "having sex." I'm disturbed by the misuse of this. I do not want people to engage in any act that they cannot do with authenticity—most particularly, when it involves the heart of another being, as well as their own.

When two people agree upon casual sex in a protected and mutually regarding way, it's not a sinful act. By using the word "sin," I mean moving truly away from one's divine self. And when it comes to making love, it doesn't just happen in a bedroom. Dear one, would you share what making love has come to mean to you?

There was a time when sex meant love, acceptance, and connection. This was in my teenage years. I wasn't receiving the actual love I needed from my family, and I had no way to ask for it. In my twenties, a strong sexual desire was present. Yet it diminished early on, much to my dismay, due to a long painful relationship with a man. All of our unresolved issues kept me from wanting him in this way.

In my early thirties, I changed three major things in my life at one time. I let go of the nine-year relationship, my New York City residence, and my career as a school counselor. At that juncture, I made a conscious decision to stay single and explore my sexuality. I enjoyed honestly stating my status to men. I also liked the nonattachment and sexual pleasure. It was a fantastic growing experience; I learned more about what I enjoyed engaging in and what I didn't—and became confident in communicating about it.

Presently, in my late thirties, I feel that abstinence is my predominant status. Making love, to me now, is about forming a life with someone. And forming a life with someone means coloring in our world together with shared values and spirit-led goals. Through my earlier sexual experiences, I have arrived at seeing lovemaking as a lifestyle. It has evolved past just an act, and is now a way of being.

Thank you for acknowledging your sexual experiences as empowering and liberating. There aren't, unfortunately, many societies that appreciate a woman's need for independence at certain times—or as a lifestyle.

Your understanding of making love, and your ability to describe it, evolved out of your courage to let go of your nine-year relationship—as well as to you offering yourself the time necessary to know who you are, without a significant other.

I want to add only one piece to your place of arrival, for yourself, and others. This is to no longer label a person a "boyfriend," "girlfriend," "partner," etc. Rather, I encourage you to refer to this fellow lifestyle practitioner as "beloved."

Dear one, let us now look at the term "intimacy." I also have a challenging time accepting the way it's accurately understood by so few people. Almost all those who pray to me know more intimately about my life than they do about their own.

"Intimacy" is not exclusively about sexual activity—as commonly thought. Sex can lead to intimacy, when two people engage in the courageous vulnerability it requires. Yet, many other activities are so very intimate. Our daily talks have been intimate. Vulnerability and courage have been offered by you—through the sharing of dreams, health concerns, and financial worries.

Intimacy cannot come without a sharing of one's own truth—completely. An intimate act can, however, take place even if no intimacy is involved. I'm encouraging those who have never looked upon intimacy in this way to start doing so—for fulfillment comes through authentic intimacy; taking a risk to be fully honest with oneself and with another.

Let it be known that, without true intimacy, your spirit will not adapt healthfully through its lifecycle. Craving will occur—and, hence, addiction. Addiction is primarily caused by trauma living inside one's spirit, or by an absence of intimacy. I ask that one now reevaluate how one experiences intimacy, in both verbal conversation and in physical relating—with oneself and with others.

Addictions. Wow. What about the genetic factor that has been researched as a cause of alcoholism?

December 11, 2009

~~~~~

Dear one, despite the genetic research in regard to alcoholism, only a small percentage of those who drink in large quantities are genetically motivated. Environmental factors are the leading cause of alcoholism. And this is also true with the majority of society's other addictions. Narcotics are, for some, addictive on the first try—while not for others. The differences between these two types of people are most often caused by differences in their life's level of intimacy.

Someone who uses drugs of any kind (including sugar, television, and caffeine), and who doesn't have an authentic relationship with both themselves and with others, is more likely to form an addiction to these substances. This is typically not the case for those who are experiencing intimacy, as I've described it.

Let it be known that addictive behavior leads not to

actual fulfillment but rather to a quiet desperation—a long-ing for intimacy and real connection.

So, instead of going to a drug, you're suggesting that we fulfill ourselves through authentic intimacy and by recognizing that we're also needing and craving more alignment with our light?

Thank you for stating it as you have. This is the case. I want to add that inviting in my spirit, as well as other supportive spirit guides, is a crucial part of fulfillment. Most people know my spirit helps and supports many different cultures and individuals. However, having an intimate relationship with them is not common at all.

One of my largest goals, through these conversations, is to change this. I want people to know I can hear their desperation. And that praying—but not listening for the answers directly, through their own knowing—will keep us from becoming intimate friends.

Letting in assistance from the spirit world offers the opportunity to receive guidance and to share openly. One can learn how to live more intimately in society, as well as with themselves, through dialoguing as you and I do and by believing in their experience. Learning to discern what is actually in one's highest good is the ultimate result.

I feel more fulfilled having intimate relationships with you and the other members of my spirit family, as I affectionately call you. I know others who don't have these relationships, and they don't speak of fulfilling lives. And then there are those who dabble but who don't pursue it with consistency. And I understand all of this. There was a time when I didn't connect consciously with spirit guides and there was also a time when I dabbled. And, although a lot of that time was painful, I trust in the necessity of it.

Interestingly enough, it is due to my relationship with you that I trust this. During this past year of intense spiritual training, I once asked you why I had to go through as many traumatic experiences as I have. You answered my question in a way that helped me feel some peace with these previous chapters in my life.

> Your testimony is illustrated by the way you are choosing to live your life. Would you now let it be known, to whatever degree you're willing, why there was previously this amount of pain in your life?

The depth of pain allowed me to get an idea of how much pain exists on the planet. It showed me how distantly we have strayed from our own core. And it showed me how most of us are not prepared to find our way home, to return to who we are.

The pain also allowed me to experience where this lost feeling can lead people, as I engaged in suicidal ideation in my twenties—and revisited this depression in my early thirties. I didn't know where to go where I would actually feel at peace. My friends offered words that had very little staying power, but it was the place I thought I should go.

Once my pain turned physical, it became unbearable. I then sought out doctors. However, Western doctors seemed to keep me spiraling, so I began seeking alternatives. I met with Eastern medical practitioners, nutritionists, body workers, and a shaman. It was she who told me my pain was my call to healing work. (It was manifesting itself by my sensitivity to many things in the environment, and feeling unwell because of them.) She was actually the third practitioner to tell me this, but she was the first one who had experienced all the same symptoms. She said they had come to her "in order to get her attention."

I continued my journey, after working with her, from a stronger place. I stopped feeling broken, and began to feel encouraged. I still, however, wasn't ready to accept that "call." Two years later, I organically found my way to healing school. I needed those years to continue releasing some unhealthy elements I was allowing into my life—and to continue with my self-empowerment. I've since come to know my pain as a foundation for understanding and compassion—for myself and for others. It has also been a yellow brick road to my purpose.

Who are your spirit guides that assisted you in your arrival at healing school?

December 14, 2009

~~~~~~~

There was no single guide that I went to and dialogued with on any regular basis. I had more of a playful way. I would walk in the woods and say what I was thinking and feeling, and/or with what challenge I needed guidance. I would then wait, and listen for an answer. I trusted I would receive one, and I usually did. Sometimes I would sit by a body of water when asking. Other times I would place my hands on the exposed trunk of a tree, or on the earth, and I would ask and listen. I always felt comforted when doing this.

You had been introduced to me as my most significant guide before I entered healing school, around the time I met with the shaman. However, it was only after I entered school that I accepted your presence in my life on a consistent basis.

Rest assured, the nature spirits assisted you in seeking clarity through the elements in their environment. I also want you to now know that I was the one hearing your prayers and cries for peace, as well as your fear of the darkness within your own being. My hands held yours, despite your belief that you were utterly alone.

Would you consider letting our readers know about when you knew, for the first time, that I was your actual guide?

Yes, I've become more comfortable with the story. Yet, at first I wasn't eager to share it out of concern over being judged or misunderstood.

I was thirty-three, in upstate New York, and exploring new ways of living my life. I had befriended a fellow poet, a very unique young man. One evening we attended a "nondenominational spiritual group" at his college. The facilitator of the group led us on a guided visualization. The intention was to meet our own guide. So up the "mountain" I went, expecting to see Buddha. It wasn't him, however, and I was shocked.

It was you. You were luminous and began walking towards me. All I could think about was that you'd gotten the wrong gal. "I'm a Jew. You're not supposed to be my guide!" I said this, and yet it didn't seem to matter.

There we were, face to face, body to body, and then you stepped right into mine. We were one. I was scared. I felt that I was doing something wrong. It felt sexual, and yet not erotic. It felt invasive, but not dangerous. I tried to leave, but you kept me there with you. And then it was over. You stepped out of my energy field and told me that you had just "impregnated me with myself." You then stayed with me a little while longer, simply sharing space—and I felt comforted.

I spoke of this with the group, despite some apprehension on my part. The facilitator was excited, and my friend told me he appreciated my courage. A couple of months later, when I turned thirty-four and took a trip to Europe, I found myself

going into all the churches and listening to both you and Mary.
That was new!

Thank you, dear one, for acknowledging all your fear
around what has been deemed "appropriate" and otherwise. Much to my dismay, your society confuses what is
and isn't appropriate. However, my intention right now is
to support your decision to share your experience—both
the night it occurred, as well as in our conversation.

More people ought to know that many Jewish people
feel uncomfortable acknowledging that I existed—and do
exist now, in the form of spirit. Your birth into a Jewish family, despite what other religions may conclude, offers you
as much right as anyone to communicate with me and to
befriend me, and I with you.

I'm glad we're speaking about this. Most of the Jewish people I presently know get quiet when I speak about you. It's a rar-
ity for any of them to ask questions and encourage conversation.
However, there's another healer I know casually. She is Jewish
and says she has been in relationship with you for many years,
but that it's also not something she discusses much. Could you
shine a little light on why?

My time on earth in physical form was not long, and
was primarily misunderstood. Many of my fellow Jewish
people suffered, despite the formalized religious services
and practices. I could not bear to witness the lack of fair-
ness, unspoken infidelities, and robbing of the poor for the
sake of offering more to the ones who had enough already.
The actions I took were in response to what I heard in
prayer, from the Creators.

They asked me to improve life as we knew it. They told me how religion is supposed to serve all who believe in it—and that its primary purpose is to communicate that the Creators know and adore each individual as their own child. They told me that being a religious person means caring for one another fully, appropriately, with sanctity. This wasn't the experience of the Jewish people I knew.

I trusted what I heard, so I set out looking for those who'd want to help the new teachings be known. These people came to be termed my "disciples." However, they too truly wanted a more sacrificial and loving way of existing. I only had to qualify that our goal was teaching all those who weren't living this way.

Each person decided, on his or her own, to take part. Despite this, many Jewish people were angered that members of their families left and were out building a new religious society. Their anger generated more anger and, as you know, my intentions for equanimity, peace, and compassion amongst the people were not met.

This, dear one, is the answer to your question about why there are many Jewish people who feel they need to ignore that I ever existed—let alone that I exist now. And yet there are some who are too fearful to share that they indeed have a relationship with me. And let us not forget the Jews who want a relationship with me, but who also are too scared to do it because of society's belief of what is appropriate. I hope this will change!

Are you saying that the present feelings people have about you are residue from when you walked the earth?

Why are you surprised? Many of today's misunderstandings are rooted in a time well before the events we've discussed. And yes, I'm telling you that present prejudices and fears, in regard to me, come from when I lived on earth—when I was offering new ways of living that weren't understood. They weren't understood then, and neither were they given the proper time and trust to demonstrate their full truth.

Okay, so what can be done now to shift the relationship between you and your fellow Jews?

December 15, 2009

I encourage people to seek out the truth. Regular walking within nature—as you stated earlier—can offer people clear guidance, clarity of heart, and true knowing. Doctrine, on the other hand, despite its historic acclaim, ought to be questioned—both by those who have been preaching it, and by those who have been accepting it, as the only truth.

Most importantly, it needs to be known that I had no intention of abolishing Judaism. Rather, my purpose was to help the Jews love anew and to show them the way. Allowing my fellow Jews to suffer was not something I was willing, or able, to do. I love them now, as I loved them then. I know them as sons and daughters of the Creative Forces. May this awareness of my desire to honor who they were—and are—overshadow all the parting that was never necessary. I say this knowing the time has come to reunite.

How can those who are ready, who want a relationship with you, start the process?

> Any time anyone—Jew or non-Jew—wants to communicate with me, the invitation is there. Calling me by name and possessing a clear intention for us to have intimate knowledge of each other is all that's needed. Keeping one's heart and mind connected with one's intention will contribute strongly to the benefits of the relationship.
>
> Dear one, would you share a benefit that has resulted from communicating with me regularly, as you have?

One benefit! My whole life is more cohesive because of our relationship. It's the common thread. Your loving nature offers me a feeling of being cared for that is new. I don't feel any judgment, only assistance with the alignment of my proper path. And this sparks inspiration in me to keep traveling on it. And I make this choice not because I want to please you. Rather, I choose this because I've come to know that living this way feels right. I also don't look to you, or experience you, as a father. Yet, you're what I would consider a perfect parent.

> I welcomed your sharing so others could know the potential of living within a relationship with me. I'm delighted how your experience is so rich—and pleased that my relating with you helps you learn to trust your own choices and encourages self-actualization.
>
> I'm aware that there are teachers and religious authorities that share my teachings while instilling fear. Let this not be a deterrent to turning towards me. For one can learn an enormous amount independently and/or with me per-

sonally, by quieting the mind and truly listening, and then moving out into the world as one who knows the truth.

I'm glad you said this. I've heard friends and acquaintances share stories of the misuse of your name and teachings—especially by people in positions of authority. This, in turn, has scared them away—and they have never returned.

I, too, have my own story that I've rarely told. In college, I started getting to know a young woman, a dance major. I love to dance, so we had plenty of common ground to discuss. One day, she took out a small Bible and spoke about how it was "spiritual" and how it supported her journey. She then invited me on a retreat, after she offered her status as being a "born again Christian." I let her know I was Jewish and wasn't into Christianity. She then assured me it was a spiritual gathering—not a religious one! After a bit more assurance, I decided to go.

It was winter in New York. We took a train a few hours north of the city, and then a taxi to the hotel where the event was being held. The plan was to attend a meet-and-greet event before dinner. I couldn't imagine how I was going to meet-and-greet the Woodstock-sized crowd of young people who showed up. I didn't. I was one of the last people to arrive in the hall. I couldn't see what was going on in front, but I heard everything.

The lights went out and people started screaming—as if someone they loved had just been killed. Well, that's exactly what was being depicted. The reenactment of your crucifixion was taking place, complete with the smell of blood and no shortness of drama. My heart adopted an unfamiliar beat, and I had the feeling of being prey in a jungle of predators. In the dark, I pushed through the paralysis I was feeling and found the door. I turned toward the light, and got out.

I felt betrayed and trapped. I was at a proselytizing hoedown, miles from home, in a snowstorm, with no wheels of my own and having to share a room with a sister who lied.

I sought comfort in the gift shop, and shared my story with the saleswoman. After receiving some consoling, I made plans to leave the next morning. This trauma stayed with me for quite some time. I inwardly shut down to anything related to you.

It's fear that propagates this kind of unfortunate occurrence. All the masses of people who gather in my name to honor me—my crucifixion as well as my rebirth—needn't participate in these acts. There are only a few who understand how I serve all beings alike, not only those who form religions based on their beliefs about me. If I could choose one thing for the masses to do, it'd be for them to create peace among themselves—instead of believing that the way to create it is by fervently praying for it.

In regard to how you felt betrayed and traumatized, would you please share what turned you toward my light, after you had the experience that triggered these feelings?

December 18, 2009

〜〜〜

It was a few years after the event. I was out of college and working. It was a rare occasion, a day when New York City schools were closed due to snow. I had a free day, so I decided to paint. I went to the part of my house with four large windows, set up my easel, and placed a blank canvas on it. I had no intention other than to bring forth whatever needed birthing.

Six hours later, which I barely noticed, a female figure emerged on the canvas—with flowing hair and no visible anatomy. There were symbols in her hair representing duality. She had one eye in the middle of her forehead, and no facial details. To one side of her, the paint was very energized—like beams of light. The other side was quite still. And, in the bottom corner, there was a cross with three circles surrounding it.

The whole painting surprised me. It felt foreign to the world I knew. The cross troubled me. I thought about what my family would say if they saw it. I already felt different from them, more by the year, actually. I considered blending the oil paint into the background so the form would be unseen. But I left it for the night, knowing the paint would still be wet in the morning.

Dawn broke with the sound of my alarm. I looked at the painting by the window and decided to take the risk of leaving the cross intact. After that decision, I felt a thin connection grow between us that showed itself again from time to time. It felt gentle and unobtrusive. Most importantly, it felt real and unforced.

It's my desire to have all my relationships be organic in nature, such as ours. Your decision to not clear the cross away, and to let my contact with you remain visible, set the groundwork for all that unfolded next. It prepared the way for our relationship.

You chose to leave the cross, despite the misgivings that were induced by your upbringing and your troubling experience in college. Many would have turned away, rather than towards, me.

. You trusted yourself. Please don't disregard the significance of this. Let it be known that, regardless of all the untruths you have been exposed to, the honoring of what felt real overcame. Choosing to keep the cross illustrates how truth-seeking had, by then, become important to you.

Now, regarding your family, there was not a solid level of trust between you and them. They'd taught you that your perceptions—of yourself, them and the world—were wrong. The pain from doubting yourself became crippling to your intuition. Therefore, you didn't apply the knowing you possessed for many years.

Deciding to not blend the cross, and then showing the painting in an art show, demonstrated how you were beginning to trust your own knowing. I'm focusing on your search for truth in order to illustrate how, despite at times doubting your sense of knowing, you always had it—as do all beings that walk the earth.

What tools can you offer to assist people in developing their stronger sense of knowing—and to have trust in this knowing?

Here is an exercise one can engage in. I invite you, and all people, to think back to a time when nobody disregarded you—before you were exposed to the feeling of not being valuable. This is the time when your knowing was most readily accessible. Once this time is restored to memory, stay with the experience—allowing it to wash over you. In so doing, the feeling of your own knowing will become familiar again. When ready, move on to envisioning where the false belief of not knowing has been stored in your body. The awareness will begin to diminish the power of the false belief.

This practice is to help recapture your soul's knowing. It's important to not engage in this alone—unless you're skilled in psychotherapy, hypnotherapy, or similar healing professions. Integrating your knowing back into the way you live will create a large impact, and both you and the process deserve to be handled with care.

I'm concerned that, even though what you're suggesting is vital, it may also be esoteric for many people.

It's time to welcome in what will serve the highest good, and to no longer refuse to accept ways of healing that fall outside of what has been termed "Western medicine." I'm unhappy that it's predominantly allopathic medical practitioners who are sought after. Complementary medicine makes too small of an impact. I'm inviting all people who don't know the value of complementary health care practices to learn about them. I encourage it to become globally mainstream.

I am also going to ask Western medical doctors to be aware that their gift of providing health and healing support doesn't exclude them from seeking their own healing. Deeper levels of health can be sought. Practitioners are meant to stay balanced, practice clean health, continue self-education, and visit other balanced health care providers. One then becomes a model, an example of wellness.

Since we're on the topic, I would like it to be known that I see many contradictions within Western medicine. A large segment of the population views doctors as gods. Another large segment views the whole field as corrupt, greedy, and calloused. Promoting wellness is not to be chosen as a profession for the sake of wealth, nor ought those who practice medicine be placed above another. I'm hopeful that by bringing this all to light, the much needed changes will occur!

December 21, 2009

It's Monday and Christmas is Friday. I'm feeling moved to talk about this. Is it alright to go on to a new topic, even though I'm sure there is more to discuss regarding this one?

Know that we can always return to discussing my desire for a balanced healthcare system—one that supports, rather than depletes, society. For now, let's talk about Christmas.

Christmas, in modern society, is meant to be a Sabbath time. However, it is embellished with decorations, expensive gift buying, and excessive preparations for parties and gatherings. The cost of this is that society is neglecting to honor Christ Consciousness—both in oneself, and in one another. It is this quality of consciousness that is intended to rest at the heart of the holy season.

Let it also be known that a Sabbath is a gift for those who work long hours. It is important to take time out to rest and reflect—especially if one does not stop to do this regularly during their working days. As for relatives and friends gathering together: I suggest that this not occur as a mandatory act, as I've often seen, but rather only when each individual is inspired to participate in the gathering.

·A long time ago, when I was a young child in Nazareth, no one would come to our house during Chanukah. Rather, we spent every night of this season quietly—while each of us who lived in my home reflected on life's miracles, as they were illuminated by Chanukah's miracle of light. Each evening, we would honor all the work we did throughout the year by engaging in only necessary tasks and allowing ample time to rest.

I'm well aware how differently present societies operate. Few reflect unless they're forced to do so. My hope is to inspire people of all nations to not allow more of their lives to pass without deep reflection, for truth needs these times in order to be born.

I appreciate what you said. Last year, I took a Sabbath Christmas. After having breakfast with a friend, I went to a natural area, hiked, and listened to my inner self and to you. This year I plan on doing the same.

However, there were many years when I was quite caught up with the gifts and the gatherings. It felt inauthentic and unnatural, yet I was deep in that world. How did it begin? Or rather, why did the time for honoring your birth become stressful, forced, and expensive?

In order to know the answer, one can listen to his or her heart. It is worth investigating one's own values and belief system.

Indications of how the Spirit of Christmas has been abandoned, however, linger in the air of department stores on the evening before the birthday celebration. Tremendous sacrifices go on, all for this single day of the year. One way this happens is through the overtime work people feel compelled to do. Some take on an additional job so they'll have enough money to buy the gifts their loved ones want.

Let it be known that additional work—more than is required to fulfill one's needs and/or responsibilities—calls for energy that is not provided by the Creators. Rather, this energy is taken from the health of one's relationships, the relationship one has both with one's self and with others. No one ought to be living in such a manner. My hope is to witness people listening to their hearts about how this began, and to watch them discover new ways to celebrate my birth.

It's my hope too. Also, when something is "taken" and not returned, it is considered lost. Is this what you mean?

The issue you ask me to qualify is about compromise, which ought not be a regular part of life. Except in a courtroom, for example, when a judge reduces a sentence in exchange for the person on trial paying a sum of money.

Compromising anything compromises all those involved, regardless of whether or not they are conscious of it. This includes compromising one's soul for money. Or one's relationships, and the qualities of those relationships (and availability within them), due to the belief that material things are of greater importance. Once again, an individual may be unable to feel that a compromise is happening—but that doesn't mean that it isn't.

"Unable to feel." I believe I was once one of these people. I also have experienced this in the company of friends, family, and clients. I believe it would be valuable to hear you speak about it.

Being unable to feel is rooted in the fear that starting to feel may bring up more emotions than one can handle. People sometimes close themselves off to feelings in order to not "explode" in anger, tears, or pain of some kind. The only true way to get through the fear that creates this experience of numbness is to allow any difficult feelings to be experienced. This exercise will bring back one's sense of feeling, in a more balanced way.

This deliberate process also ought to include a skilled and compassionate professional; someone who can assist the release of the root of this terror-to-express in one's life. My hope is that working through one's fearful feelings instead of hiding them will soon be considered normal.

December 23, 2009

I've gone through multiple stages learning how to express myself. I look back to my youth and realize that, like many children, I was terrorized and conditioned to stay quiet by fear of punishment, rejection, and blame.

I've cleared a lot of that through psychotherapy and energy healing. Yet, I still consistently work with my own inner "terrorizer"—because she took over the job. She is the judge, the saboteur, and the recluse. She has become more easy-going, but we've had some difficult times. Being aware of her helps me to calm her. And being conscious of the necessity of expressing myself helps me work through any new and/or residual fear around doing so.

As you have indicated, working through fear in order to share one's heart and truth can also occur independently. This can happen after one has acquired training; through teachings from those who have gone before and know how to do this work.

I encourage anyone who wants to work through their fear of expressing themselves to do so; to no longer allow the death of their character, purpose, and true happiness to occur. Rather, fear the fear continuing—for it's a greater risk to live without true expression and the sense of freedom that it brings.

I would now like to talk about money. I bring this up because there are two days left until Christmas and money is driving most people's thoughts, behaviors, and what are believed to be life-enhancing plans. However, my joy would be for high-priced ticket items to no longer be given away in my name. Rather, my hope is that those who have a lot of money will consider those who have much less of it—by offering help and support. I'm suggesting people give for the sole purpose of acting as a creative force in the universe. For this is the point of it all. Giving is a way to not forget.

By cultivating this Christ consciousness, people can come to know how it feels to be Christed and how it is available to them as a way of daily life—not solely on my birthday.

When I hear you use the term "Christed," I think of Leonardo Da Vinci. I remember learning in college that "Vinci" is actually the area in Italy where Leonardo was from, rather than his last name—which is unknown. I believe many people think of "Christ" as your last name, as opposed to an earned status. Could you comment on this?

I not only want to comment, I also wish to discuss why people use the term when they're angry or disgusted—when experiencing a troubling circumstance. First, when considering my name, I would like "Jesus Christ" to no longer be used—for it is not my last name. Rather, I prefer "Jesus the Christed." This is not only most accurate in its description, but it allows others to be aware that they too could assume the role.

Now, let's reflect on the use of my name. I so often hear people say it in vain. Although I forgive them, my heart bleeds for their lack of connectedness to my, and their own, divinity. Let it be known that the sacredness in all life forms continues to suffer, when the sacredness lies disrespected in one by another. Therefore, my hope is that no one's name ever be said in vain.

This resonates deeply for me, and also, by the way you've expressed it, movies pop into my head. Lately, I've been noticing how regularly you're referenced—and, most often, in vain. Something shocking or terrible happens, and the actor says "Jesus Christ!" I'm confused by this. Would you be able to shed any light? I mean, can you offer any understanding you may have about it?

My name is used in this context in films, for the same reason I just gave to you. It's the speaker's lack of connection to my, and his or her own, divinity. And now a new topic is coming up for discussion. It's the fact that art influences large groups of people. And much to my dismay, exhibiting one's "rights"—as opposed to creating what's in the highest good for all—is the focus more often than not.

December 24, 2009

You were beginning to discuss the influence of art yesterday. Would you like to continue with that?

Yes, I would. A long time ago, some of my disciples explored an artistic lifestyle consisting of drawing, singing, painting, and dance. My offering to them, in order to have divine energy fuel their art, was to encourage them to not allow the truth of their gifts to be forgotten by their desire to become known.

When one creates what they are being called to bring forth, it will inevitably be for more people than only themselves. It is meant to be shared. I ask all the artists of today to consider the personal and societal responsibility inherent in their role.

I've felt, recently, a sacredness in the art I create. I have created it by purely allowing it to flow through me—without editing it or forcing it to go in a desired direction. Times when I've set out with a clear intention to create, but without checking in with my own intuition or spirit guides, I felt blocked in sharing it after I finished it. I presently feel most interest in sharing any art that has been a conscious co-creation.

I know your sole intention for co-creating your art is to not stray away from what is real. My hope is that co-creating, and allowing one's spirit to drive one's art, will become the new inspiration behind such an important part of earthly society. Clearing away one's ego, so one's spirit can hear itself and the spirit world, can only infuse art with its true intention, the intention to change thinking and affect behavior for the good of all.

What would be something you would like to see created as art? Or, is there something that has already been created that you appreciate?

When it comes to art, there are many forms—as well as specific creations—that I enjoy. One is Walt Whitman's poetry. It illuminates life on earth in the way that it's intended. Breath, grass, and beauty are spoken about with ease and deep tenderness. *Leaves of Grass* brings joy to many. Knowing this brings me joy.

My heart celebrates each time soulful art is created for all to share and to know intimately. For it is an important way to remember one's identity as fellow creator. Great dedication is required in order to not float through life not knowing who one is. Art can illuminate life's questions, remind people who they are and inspire new works of art.

This, dear one, is the art I want to more often feel, see, and enjoy.

Is there anything in particular you would like to see teachers and/or parents doing to encourage the creation of this intuitive spirit-driven art? Beginning the encouragement early in a child's life, I imagine, would be highly beneficial.

Children need freedom without judgment! Using words other than "good" and "bad" is where teachers and parents can start reviving . . . revising. You would call that a Freudian Slip; ha, ha, ha!

Judgment words break down a child's creative freedom and, hence, their truth; their knowing. No matter how a child's work of art appears, it is more appropriate to use other phrases when responding to it, such as, "how positively divine!" For if it has been created without holding back, and without fear or a teacher or parent's commentary, then it is indeed positively divine!

Another avenue one can take, when encouraging children to create freely, is to not cap their uniqueness. For example, purple horses needn't be discouraged if it is a child's natural inclination. The damage an adult does to a child, by fearing their unique ways instead of supporting them, is highly significant and often irreversible.

Also, let's consider the effect parents can have when they disagree with each other in front of their children. When they do so with clarity and skill, they create a feeling of safety within a child. He or she is then free to create wholeheartedly, as long as the parents do not interfere with the child's unique way.

On the other hand, parents who fight and argue in

front of a child, or even behind closed doors, are establishing an unsafe environment for a child to feel present enough to create. In most cases, he or she won't express themselves artistically at all or until they are much older. And, when they do pursue it, it will tend to be for self-soothing purposes rather than co-creative.

I would like to talk now about how to really love a child. Children are not capable of forgetting how they were ill treated. Nor should they. They grow up determined not to repeat what they know didn't feel right to them. Despite their intention, more often than not, it is exactly these unwanted traits in behavior that get repeated.

Properly loving a child can bring closure to repetitive cycles in families. Loving a child carefully usually leads to loving one's self in the same way. In turn, healthier relating occurs. Loving children properly does not mean always letting them do what they want to do. Nor does it mean saying "yes" all the time. Learning how to say "no" lovingly, clearly, and with assurance, supports the development of healthy boundaries. It also offers modeling for children, which is crucial during the years when they seek to discover what ought and ought not be explored.

One thing to say "no" to is excessiveness. Allowing children more than a balanced amount of anything creates a need to control, rather than freedom for them to know. Encouraging a balance of the time spent on various activities supports learning to naturally move from one task to another—without the need for unnatural time clocks. This allows for the whole person to develop.

True balance comes with learning who one is, with the experience of having tried other ways and finally coming to sense what is "right" through the feeling in one's body.

Teaching children not only about balance, but also about how to know what feels right in their bodies, would be a sure way to properly love them.

The last issue I want to speak about on this topic is dangerous relationships with friends: relationships where loss of self-esteem or well-being is at stake. The fact is, unhappiness pervades many schools and leads some students to develop unhealthy ways of coping.

One thing that contributes to this dynamic is a child's loss of a parent, or a child maturing without even having met his or her parent. This can create a sense of darkness. Often, this causes a build-up of unexpressed feelings to form that later emerge in unproductive and dangerous ways. One reason children form friendships is to repeat mother, father, and sibling relationships. Children often come together unconsciously to work through any unresolved issues. This can create bonds that are threatening to seemingly small traits in a child's character and can severely damage his or her emotional well-being. The type of friendship I'm referring to is with children who torment others because they themselves have been tormented. A consistent withdrawal, alternating with insincere friendship, is an example of this. Additional unresolved issues may be acted out and merit careful attention. Mindfulness while parenting, as well as heart-fullness, allows both child and parent to be loved properly.

December 29, 2009

How was Christmas for you?

I feel I spent this day in the best way I could under the circumstances, given that I don't want to be in Virginia anymore. After spending the morning resting and reflecting, I had my dearest local friend over and made a meal—to honor both the anniversary of your birth and his support over the last few months.

Why do you stay somewhere you no longer want to be?

My intuition, as well as the spirit guides with whom I communicate (including you) have led me to believe I'd best not move on to the next place yet.

What causes your determination to resist going against these forces, and to not pick up and leave?

Quite frankly, I'm dedicated to this project with you. It feels like the most meaningful way I could be spending my time, helping you share your messages. What I've also come to realize is that being somewhere I'd rather not be, during the cold winter, allows me to focus on this manuscript. I have no interest in going out, or in seeing or doing anything else.

As I share with you, I'm realizing another significant thing: This is simply now what I do! I listen to the forces and do whatever is in the highest good, despite whether or not it's my preference.

I'm enjoying how all your decisions are based on what you feel and believe are for the highest good of all. Your ability to trust both yourself and your communication with your spirit family came through trials—and yet you continue, again and again, to keep clear communication one of your major priorities.

Thank you for your acknowledgement. It has been a difficult path, and also truly fulfilling.

On a less amenable note . . . I'd like to now move on to discuss politics. My wish is that a person's integrity, character strength, and determination be the reasons to elect any political figure. When this isn't the case, only challenges will occur. Challenges of greater and greater magnitude are unfolding, due to cavalier thinking by elected officials. Many of those legally bound in government, to act for the highest good of all people, stray away from this. Selfish displays and corrupt interaction lies beneath, and around, many government acts.

I am now calling on the individual spirits who remain trapped inside these people, as well as the ones who vote them into office, to know that it is possible to live by more truth. Indeed, it is necessary. The fear that keeps these individuals from their truth doesn't need to exist. It sprouts from their belief that they are not enough, and there isn't enough—in general.

This belief in scarcity undermines societies as a whole. All these misconceptions could be let go of with the knowledge that each being is created with exactly what it needs. Then these beings would be free to enjoy their lives rather than squandering them.

Let us now look at how these misconceptions occur. Many individuals live passively. Someone has created an outline that they believe they need to follow. The outline allows little or no consideration for what they feel or want. Rather, the concerns are about the role, the title, the pay, and the prestige. Originality, otherwise known as one's original essence, is rarely honored.

Scarcity is usually considered to be not having sufficient time, money, or belongings. However, it is truly about not having one's self! Politics is so vast that it creates an opportunity for people to fail to examine their own lives and evaluate them for authenticity. Instead, they become overly focused on those in the spotlight—a decoy, a distraction. Inevitably distraction will lead, and has always led, to more distraction. This turns people farther and farther away from their original selves.

The simple solution is to not fear one's original self. Rather, be curious. Another part of the solution is for each person to decide what he or she wants, despite whether or not it currently exists for him or her. And lastly, the solution means letting go of the belief that the Creative Forces must have been wrong when it came time to bring "you" into the world.

Thank you for speaking so clearly. I know this information will be quite valuable. I'm currently engaged in not only discerning my original self from my conditioning, but I'm also learning to trust her. I have already been using what you suggested as a mantra, the part about the creative forces not being "wrong."

For me, this also comes back to authentic expression. I have been engaging in, and practicing, authentically expressing myself for years. The fear of doing so runs deep. There are a lot of layers. I have pushed through many. I'm also sensing that I'm being called to go to a whole new level of expression. It's a place that feels a little uncomfortable for me. I'm being asked to be verbal with my knowing outside of the healing studio and workshop setting.

I'm feeling two challenges come up for me around this. One is that I have worked deliberately on quieting my ego and keeping my unsolicited commentary and advice to myself. This new level of authentically expressing myself is about stepping up and saying what is coming through me. I know now it wouldn't be about ego satisfaction, but rather about offering what someone needs. However, I have yet to embrace the authority I've been given.

This leads to the second challenge. I'm simply not yet comfortable being in this role. Perhaps it's because it's foreign to me. I imagine the discomfort also has to do with my belief that I'll lose friends by no longer holding my breath and playing a more quiet, compassionate role.

Ah, yes. In order to attain this new level of authority, you are indeed being asked to claim, and act upon, the truth as you know it. You have to let go of the fear of hurting anyone's feelings or losing your friends. To embrace your own evolution, quietness has to be released.

It's not in the highest good to fear sharing what you know to be true when it comes to the well-being of people, places, and things. There ought not be judgment coming through you towards anyone—only seeing, and then sharing. Continuing to keep your human-made ego out of your new role is vitally important. This calling need not be feared. All you have completed before now has readied you.

December 30, 2009

Today I'd like to talk about the time I walked the earth in flesh. I'll begin by saying I had only one male friend. Despite my many followers, disciples, and those who wanted and/ or needed my service, he was the closest to me.

Judas, otherwise known as the only disciple who betrayed me, was actually the only one who did not. Although there are people who will already know what I'm going to share through their having been exposed to the gospel of Judas, there are more who would never have heard it. Let it be known that I confirm that which the gospel claims about my death having been pre-planned by both Judas and me to be true. I want this to be known to clear Judas' name, to illuminate the nature of our relationship, both then and now, and to clarify what was required of me during this time: It was to not be bound by skin, blood, and bones—but rather to be freed to reside in the realm of the spirit, so as to assist all of those who would otherwise be inaccessible to me.

Judas, unlike all the other disciples, did not fear me. Rather, his only fear was not serving his God. Knowing this, he and I became confidants. I shared my mission with him: to serve the many instead of only a few. Upon hearing this, he requested to serve in any way that would be possible. Judas and I then planned what later became known as his betrayal of me. I want his intentions to be known. For now Judas has the status of saint. And he has always lived close to me, spirit to spirit.

Let it be known that this information comes not to challenge, but rather as an opportunity. What would now serve the religions based on what are thought to be my beliefs, and teachings, would be for them to evolve into accepting the new information. For it shows what I believed before the religions were created, and believe even more strongly now: that one must do what's in the highest good for all.

Therefore, any and all consequences ought to be of a human spirit-broadening nature that spans the globe. Dear children of Creation, there need not be fear of change. Evolution is destined.

This is huge news, about Judas not being someone who betrayed you—and that you planned your own death. I'm glad you spoke on how you would like this to be received by people. I know I'm surprised, and also intrigued. And yet it feels right, now that I've heard it. It also inspires me to ask you about friendship— yet I hesitate to move on now, having heard about you and Judas.

One must always move on. This is precisely one of my main points. And, to speak now about friendship—this seems fitting. I encourage people to evaluate their own friendships. Are they anchored in trust—the kind of trust where difficult things can be spoken, despite fear of the outcome truth may create? Can one or the other change into who they are supposed to be, without it being cause for ridicule—either subtle or overt? And, can both people sustain autonomy and continue developing interpersonal intimacy?

Please begin to ask these questions, if you're not already doing so. Knowing the truth can be comforting, rather than inducing a sense of loneliness. Truth, in any situation, creates freedom, freedom for whatever is best for all involved to appear at its destined time. I highly encourage people to believe more in this doctrine than in their conditioned fear.

It sounds like a perfect recipe for friendship: bringing forth the truth and letting go of fear, allowing destiny to do the rest. You did mention destiny.

Ah, destiny. Yes, I mentioned it. Undoubtedly, it's one of the topics most questioned, debated, and philosophized about on planet earth. But let it be known that destiny merits even more earthly attention! Destiny is at the heart of the truth of all things. And this truth is that every one on your planet has a divined purpose that is destined!

In order to understand destiny, however, one needs to abandon the myth that every thing in one's life is destined. Choice exists—as does destiny. For example, a person may be destined to be an artist. However, the choices this person makes determine how this will be established. One can choose direct and deliberate paths by seeking out truth; paths that will keep him or her closely aligned with his or her destined purpose. Or, as has been so often illustrated throughout many existing societies, this same person can believe in falseness and engage in many unsupportive things; things that will keep him or her from fully actualizing his or her destiny, or sadly missing it entirely.

Would you talk about what you mean by unsupportive things?

One of the things I am referring to is watching television, where there is very little worthy of one's divine energy—and it is indeed divine energy that people are spending on it. Divine energy needs like energy in order to prosper; in order to see one's full potential.

Another unsupportive activity is glorifying professional sports. Highly paid professional game-playing is about showmanship. And showmanship truly does not support society's basic need for sportsmanship. Someone who displays sportsmanship to others offers genuine goodwill, no matter if they're being paid or not.

Professional sports not only spend a lot of money that could be better used elsewhere, it also dilutes the point of a game. The point, as I understand it, is supposed to be accessible and lighthearted fun for those who are participating and for those involved as spectators. I realize my opinion on this will potentially be unpopular. However, anyone who is willing to be alone and quiet with this for a little bit of time may also come to recognize the truth of what I've just expressed.

Continuing to answer your question, another unsupportive activity is shopping for merchandise other than what one knows is right for him or her—other than what one truly wants or needs. Browsing malls or websites is simply spending time with no greater purpose.

I want to directly illuminate time's preciousness. I urge all the sons and daughters of the Creative Forces to not waste time. I encourage them to deliberately choose whether they're going to act in alignment with their destiny or with continued falseness.

I appreciate your answer, despite its "potential" unpopularity. And illuminating destiny and choice feels really important. I'd like to hear now about your destiny.

Your curiosity invokes a new topic and one I need to address in order to respond fully: past lives. There are some people who do not agree with this idea of having many lifetimes. Let it be known, however, that there are past and future lifetimes.

A person lives many times in order to continue evolving into who they are destined to become—their spirit's essence. What has been created this lifetime is what's needed to be worked through, anything in the way, anything needing resolution.

Now in regard to my destiny, I have lived many lifetimes in order to become who I am now. I even lived a lifetime where I wasn't at all nice or pleasing to others. It was one where I needed to repeat some prime issues before I became close to a spirit-driven life.

And now, let it be known that I have reached my destiny. I am exactly who the Creators had planned for me to be. And so are some earth-bound people almost ready for their own passage; for the full evolution of their destiny.

For instance, when a young person dies, it's often that

their spirit is ready to be fully and completely engaged in their destined purpose. I know how most people feel a young person dying is unacceptable. I assure you that, unless they are indeed ready for their destined purpose, what will occur upon their death is another life experience—a lifetime that helps move them toward all that is waiting for them! Death, therefore, needn't be feared as happening prematurely.

My intention is for death to be understood as a divinely purposeful event . . . one that is necessary and okay. I encourage people to visit this perspective in quietude, so any personal disbelief and discomfort can be acknowledged. And hopefully moved through.

When I hear you speak about "quietude" for regarding your messages, and sitting with any questions and/or discomfort, it makes me wonder if you're prescribing meditation.

Meditation helps create the space where one can hear truth, or cherish the silence. Let it be known that in order to actually ground into one's being, as a tree does into the earth, one needs time for utter quiet and stillness. So "prescribing meditation," although I have not considered it before, is precisely what I'm going to do. And I recommend it be done for at least twenty minutes each day.

My journey with meditation has been long and lean. During my days of studying Buddhism, there was allocated meditation time in each class—and I loved it. The depth of relaxation and groundedness I felt was unique from the way I experienced the rest of my life. I tried to keep this going when I stopped attending classes, but I was not able to do so with regularity.

My present daily ritual includes quiet stillness, listening, and reflection. However, I have been yearning to experience more silence. This seed ripened very recently. I'm now sitting once a day with the intention of enjoying the space in between the thoughts.

This activity is showing me I don't have to chase after the chatter that goes through my head. Also, when I'm not consciously sitting in meditation, but involved with the day's other engagements, I still have this awareness. When I'm able to abide in that space of non-thinking, everything feels less emotionally charged and simply better. And a couple times it seemed as if I could feel my body being held up by a cloud.

In order to assist people in committing to your prescription, what can you offer them, for this is not an easy activity?

January 1, 2010

The first thing one can do is to not waste time philoso-
phizing about whether or not meditation works to calm a
person's mind. One can only come to a conclusion about
its effectiveness by practicing it. Also, let go of the need
for conditions such as a place perfect with bright light,
candles lit in front of a vase of fresh flowers, and a fluffy
sitting cushion. They are not necessary for silent stillness to
take place. Although meditation does require quiet, it does
not require ambience. And yet, if it's desired and possible,
allowing ambience to assist in opening one to a daily ritual
and committed practice—then, I say, why not!

I ask that anyone who wants to try meditating, to sit in
silence one time a day. Begin with five to ten minutes. Once
one feels relaxation and knows peace, I believe that they
will want to continue, increasing both the duration and the
frequency of their practice. Even though one will not ini-

tially be able to fully clear their mind, one needs to know that this will happen in time.

I encourage embracing commitment to this activity that brings one closer to knowing who and what they are—and doing this will be easy when one recognizes the priceless gifts that come through that awareness.

How do you remain clear in mind and spirit? Is there meditation in your realm?

Meditation does exit in the spirit realm; it's an activity enjoyed by many. Although I rarely do it, I know how it helped me when I needed it. Now, I clear my energy through ocean air. Spirits from all walks go to beaches across this planet to clear their energy field. For it's sand and the ocean, along with an endless horizon, that supports us more than meditation.

This need for different methods is due to how much humans think. We, as spirits, do not think. Therefore, we only need to clear our energy field. However, I'm solely speaking from the spirit realm in which I am bound. Spirits who are in transition, and looking for asylum, are in a whole different realm. And, it's due primarily to their thinking that they have not yet circled back to the place from whence they came.

The non-thinking leaves one's channels clear. It allows one to hear all that ought to be heard. One becomes more available; more able to hear spirit-driven guidance. Letting this occur, one's own spirit can also be deeply felt.

When I meditate, it inspires my desire for good health. And it offers me a stronger sense of calm when dealing with human-made challenges to good health. May we now speak of this important issue: that of health and the environment. This includes air quality and the environment—both outdoor and indoor—which gets overlooked by quite a large population.

> Dear one, let it be known that poor air quality imperils so many creatures' health—in addition to that of human-kind. So I'm most pleased that you're inspired to ask me about it. However, would you first state why you personally feel as passionate about clean air as you do.

Many years ago, I created art without considering the exposure to the toxicity of glues and paints—and to their corresponding environmental hazards. One day I had to stop. I stopped doing my art in the free way that I had been. I started to feel sick around chemicals of all varieties.

I then began evaluating all the ways I was ingesting toxic chemicals. What I discovered was a list so long that I chose to move and change my lifestyle. I left New York City air—which consisted of automobile exhaust, post-911 debris, and other chemicals that one would find in a densely populated city.

I stopped using commercial detergents. I changed from paraffin candles made out of petroleum to soy or beeswax. I got rid of all my furniture and bedding that had been scotch-guarded, due to the use of formaldehyde and such flame-retardants. I was furious at all of the surprises. I felt I was in the dark about products that made up my life—things that I'd believed were not only not going to harm me, but were positive additions.

> Dear one, it sounds as though your challenge was also the greatest gift you had received in quite some time. It inspired your location and career change. In addition, you

received all this new and highly significant information about how and why people, animals, trees, and ocean creatures are falling ill.

What you shared, and its importance for the direction of your own journey, is also incredibly pertinent for those who have not yet entered this way of educating themselves on healthier living—which you all have termed "green."

Many people now, who consider themselves experts in the field of healthy air quality, ought not to be followed as if they are shepherds. Rather, there are many magazines, books, Internet sites, and specialists who are humble and also knowledgeable. They are resources that help encourage this much-needed change for our global-community.

January 4, 2010

How was your New Year's weekend, dear one? Would you care to share some aspect of it that feels important?

Yeah, I feel as though I took good care of myself. And that is important to me. I didn't always understand that there are many levels of self-care—some are obvious, others subtle. And, all of these matter.

In preparation for resting this weekend, I made sure I tended to chores before the week's end. I did my laundry, got all the groceries I needed, paid bills, and returned calls. The commitment to writing your messages, in addition to working with my clients, has assisted me in making sure I put as much care into myself as I do for others. It feels like a new and deeper level of showing up. I actually like caring for myself instead of feeling fearful about what would happen if I didn't.

Before I started seeing everything as energy, I didn't believe the small things mattered to health and well-being. I thought maybe I was being a "perfectionist" or an "idealist." These were some of the labels placed on me when I voiced my preferences—which I've now come to recognize have a direct connection to my intuition.

I'm pleased you're finding greater satisfaction in your self-care. I know it has not always been this way. Not only you, but most people as well, struggle with consistency when it comes to well-being protocols. I'm curious whether you would be willing to share some of your routines—though of course nothing too personal.

You know saying no to you is rare. So . . . I'll share "some." In the morning, I clear my sinuses by using a netti pot. This helps me breathe well. I take supplements, exercise, and do yoga on specific days. I drink plenty of water and eat organic food daily. And I schedule a Sabbath day once a week, where I turn off my phone and spend the day at home—doing what feels right.

Are you also enjoying the time you're spending on activities, and with people?

Yes, more and more. However, my tastes have changed drastically. Most activities and forms of entertainment that used to appeal to me no longer have the same draw. I also find myself alone a lot. I don't feel a resonance with many people.

You have the ability to know and trust when it's time for certain forms of entertainment, and particular relationships with people, to whither away. So does everyone else. I want people to know they are not supposed to be friends with anyone for any longer than is destined. The same is true when it comes to what one likes in the way of activities. One would find great joy in more freely allowing relationships and preferences to flow in and out of their lives. Knowing this will assist in one's ability to enjoy the journey.

Are you aware of what may be enjoyable to you now?

As I think about it, it has to do with the intention of whatever is being experienced. I still enjoy sharing a meal or a cup of tea out with someone, yet now there has to be a knowing between us that anything happening outside of us is a reflection of what's happening inside of us. In other words, their relationship with spirit needs to be similar to mine in order for me to enjoy the time we share—because it's the most important part of my life. This is also now how I enjoy things alone. I still like to hike and see movies. But now I'm approaching these activities as a way to connect more with my spirit and the angelic realm.

I'm happy that you have expressed yourself. I appreciate that, even though there seems to be a feeling of aloneness in your life's present circumstances, you are still pursuing your path with diligence—without envying those who don't live their lives revolved around matters of spirit.

The angelic realm you mentioned offers consoling and companionship when one feels alone. You and others receive this abundantly. I want to share a short story of a time in which you were comforted in this way. You don't know about this choreographed event, so you will hear about it now for the first time:

You were twenty-one and on your way back to New York after your three years of studying in Arizona. A former boyfriend called you right before you were supposed to leave town. Knowing this person would potentially have a negative influence on you, an angel cleared his name and number from your answering machine. He mailed a letter after he didn't hear back from you, and it was "lost" in transit so as to never reach you.

Despite your tenacity to go back to New York City in order to get to know your father, David could have severely altered your plans. So, know that even before you began to consciously work with angels, and your designated one in particular, they were already working with you for your highest good.

Be aware that some angels can be known in spirit form and others can be known in the physical realm. To fully know them, one only needs to believe. I will now close today's time together by offering a mantra prayer—a short song to not only assist in one's growing belief, but also to call the angels closer to one's life:

"You are here now and forever,

Touching my life with all its pain and pleasure.

Shine on me with truth and glory

As your wings flutter, so do the pages of my story."

January 6, 2010

I want it to be known, dear one, that while you and I did not compose yesterday in our written conversations, we still communicated. Would you consider letting others know how we achieve this?

I spend about an hour clearing myself in the morning in order to hear you. I begin in my healing studio. I light a candle by a photograph of you. I then sit in my meditation chair, which is directed toward the altar. I visualize my energy field releasing anything unsupportive. I do this with intention and assistance from my spirit family. After I feel clear of any foreign energy, I welcome in a high vibration white light through my crown. I then ask mother earth to send up her energy through me. When I feel a sense of completion, I am then ready to listen. At this point, my highest self is communicating with you.

I first await anything you want me to know. And then, if I have any questions or concerns, I pose them and receive your input. I intuit when this process is over. The initial clearing practice plays a large role in being able to continue communicating casually throughout the day.

I'm pleased with the information you brought forth. I know it's not so comfortable for you to share intimately about the way you live. My hope is for more people to look to my spirit for assistance—for this is the sole purpose of my continued existence. I very much want those who do not know my love to ask for it in their own way—and then to be available to receive this love with an open mind and an open heart.

Let it be known, however, that I am not a wish-granter—in cases where someone wants something that is not in the highest good for that person and everyone else. One needs to know the great value in what can be received, when what they have wished for is not granted in exactly the way they envisioned it. Then they won't miss the opportunity to learn about what is truly needed. This, in turn, will also create trust—not only in their relationship with me, but also with themselves.

Let us now move onto prayer, a topic in need of attention, in order to have it be known in the way it is intended. Often children are taught to not wish for anything other than health and happiness for their loved ones. When these children grow older and become adults, many of their prayers become hopes for themselves. What I want to be known is that there isn't a need to pray for oneself. People have the potential to get what they want. Yet, it is knowing that all that has come, and all that will come, is determined by how closely one is aligned with his or her purpose.

Rather, it is necessary to instill in today's youth the importance of offering prayers to those unknown and in need. I am speaking especially of people who are dying; far from anyone they know who can care for them, and/or lost souls yearning for clarity and spiritual connection with another person. I'm speaking also of.all people and animals without adequate food, shelter, and clean drinking water. These are the ones who need our prayers ... because all are our sisters and brothers.

Hearing what you're saying resounds in my being. It reminds me of a movie on Mother Theresa that I watched this past weekend. I was moved, unexpectedly, by learning about her depth. I cried because of her integrity in all her interactions, and the trust she exhibited in hearing you. I cried because the truth of her actions was so real and my body recognized this. This emotional resonance due to witnessing another was a rare experience for me. I later learned, that same weekend, that Mother Theresa was actually the reincarnation of Mary of Nazareth—your mother. I was quite awestruck upon you sharing this with me. And yet again when I heard it, it felt right—in my body. I know you wanted me to mention this. I imagine you'll speak about why it is significant. I must admit it feels a bit uncomfortable to be the bearer of such important information.

Thank you for consistently going places that are new and often uncomfortable. You do this in the name of faithfulness to our relationship and to your destined purpose. Having said that, I'll now speak on why Mother Theresa's soul's identity was unrecognized until now.

Our Mother Mary loves all creatures and life forms. For her, it was not enough to work solely in the spirit realm. I'm not saying that I and other spirits do not love as deeply as she does. But I am saying that her spirit felt very strongly about incarnating back into human form in order to awaken as many people as possible to the pain, injustice, and suffering on the planet.

Before her arrival, no one had been addressing the needs of the sick and dying in India to the degree that was necessary. Due to the values she modeled, an enormous amount of people all over the globe were assisted in their dire circumstances. And something extraordinary occurred: those who needed to awaken and start helping . . . did! People rose to their divinity. Many, many people acknowledged their own light and volunteered time, services, skills, finances, supplies, and love. Those helping recognized that those receiving help were their soul brothers and sisters—and vice versa.

The time has come again for all the true teachers on the planet to show their substance, so that everyone can be reminded that they are divine light. Gandhi did not leave the planet without letting his power be known. Neither did Martin Luther King, Jr. Neither did Elijah the prophet. Following in the carved footsteps of past and present, soul-purpose-driven teachers are expected; it is the destiny and purpose of some people. Others are destined to carve out a new road, to assist in the awakening of one's spirit to itself.

The most important personal prayer an individual can make is the request that he or she will be able to clearly know his or her destiny. My prayers consist mostly of this. For if answered, not as many new teachers would be necessary. Rather, harmonious living would already be a reality. This is actually what we had envisioned for all of you.

Today I will leave our conversation by offering you

and all our friends another mantra prayer to sing aloud or
silently—perhaps even online at Starbucks:

"Oh let me hear of all I am.

Oh let me view myself in them.

When we know all our light

There will be no more fear or fight."

January 7, 2010

⸺⸺⸺

I sat down to write with my intention set, as usual, to hear Jesus clearly—so that I could relay whatever it was that he wanted to share with all of us. Something felt different. The only new physical change was a lamp I had placed on the desk to illuminate the pages. I cleared my head and listened. He showed up within a couple of minutes, behind me. I sensed, and saw, him taking things out of my head. He then entered into it. We became one for a short time. Then, he exited and walked to the corner of my room and started pulling out what appeared to be entities—people. This was a familiar scene to me, from my healing sessions with clients, who often need to have other people's energy removed from them. I was surprised, however, because I'm diligent about making sure my space is clear. Within a few moments, I understood what he was showing me. It was what Jesus wanted to discuss today.

You see, the corner of my room is where my mirror leans between two walls. What he was releasing were all the images that contained fear, judgment, and doubt about how I looked—both to myself and to others. This is a universal message, and it's a topic in which he wanted to share his feelings.

> Dear one, thank you for your lovely introduction for today's topic. And, thank you for acknowledging your doubt about your external beauty. I am sorry to say it is not a minor issue. It is actually hugely pervasive. Offering any insights you have received during your journey with it would be welcomed and appreciated.

Just when I thought I could keep quiet for a little while . . . I should have known. I received my wake-up call regarding external beauty as early as my junior year in high school. I went through a windshield due to a car accident. Besides all the physical traumas and wounds, I had to get *thirty-three* stitches on my face near my chin. You see, I was brought up by parents who valued external beauty tremendously. After the accident, I struggled with lowered self-confidence, believing that the thing that made me most valuable was gone.

My insights didn't start developing then, but my shift away from focusing on external beauty did. I evolved past make-up, heels, and tight clothes and began dating guys who were good people, even if they didn't move me with their own outer beauty. Varied insights came trickling in over the years. I felt I had gotten past the effect of society's—and my parents'—instilled beliefs.

Then, at around age thirty, this person came along that I liked and desired to befriend. Yet, I found him physically so unattractive that it became my focus. I then chose to deconstruct my perception of beauty in order to get to a new place. The person I'm referring to turned out to be one of my dearest friends, and only moving out of state changed our connection. This was such an important passage for me. It's no longer about ugly versus pretty. Now, common values, strength of character, integrity, kindness, and generosity are all ways of being beautiful in my eyes.

And, in regard to how I view myself: Slowly, I have come to recognize that I possess all of the above-mentioned descriptions of beauty. They continue to grow more familiar, and play an even larger role in how I see myself. However, the silver coming into my brown mane, and the faded but still visible scars, challenge me from time to time. And yet I'm still able to see the details of lines, forms, and colors as the Creators' artwork—in each individual.

Personal evolution beckons the truth, and encourages the falseness to fade away. And so, this occurred for you. The accident in your teens became quite an important milestone to redirect you.

Youth today also need redirection and ought not believe the highly unfruitful television shows and music videos that illustrate external beauty as being important. For, no matter how often children are told how beautiful or handsome they are, this will not make them strong enough to stand where strength is required. It will not give them sufficient confidence to walk through life feeling sure of their identity.

Today's young people need to learn about strength of character; how it is formed, and that it is beautiful. Let it be known that allowing one's unique beauty to shine through shows the depths of one's character.

Adults have their own journey when it comes to how they see themselves, and how they view others. I witness so much pain throughout the many lands that illustrate how this is so. It's these outer shells that enliven each soul's personality, and limit them as well. The whole reason each individual person looks unlike any other is so that their unique life's purpose can be known to them most easily.

Souls are meant to be attracted to a particular partner, place, career, and friend in order to align with their purpose. For most, this is not happening. Instead it is money, a false sense of power, religion, and fear that are wrongly attracting people to each other—with comparison being at the heart of it all.

The truth is that nothing is more beautiful or perfect than anything else—although I know the idea of comparison is highly regarded in many cultures. What I would like people to know is that something is not meant to be considered ugly so that something else can be considered beautiful. Light is meant to be appreciated all by itself, without the need to compare it to darkness. So is rain meant to be appreciated alone, without the appreciation being contingent on the promise of the sun coming through. Let it be that all the Creators' children know themselves to be beautiful—without any need for qualifiers.

January 8, 2010

I now want to address your questions. I already am aware of one in particular, and I would like to begin today by answering it. You are wondering how I can be in more than one place at a time.

Yes, I am. Although I've been accepting the fact that you're able to be in multiple places at once, I've never discussed it with you. The reason I've accepted it is due to our consistent time together, unfettered, when I am sure other people are vying for your time—and some of them are in desperate need of it. You wouldn't solely be with me and not be with them.

I truly appreciate your loyalty, despite my inability to be solely with you. Trusting my sincerity about my love for you is also a gift. Wanting to possess someone is largely popular on planet earth. Most people are not able to share their love intimately with another when they know the other is involved deeply with many people and places—fulfilling their mission.

Friendship, when it's between one person with a time-consuming purpose and someone else who has not realized his or her purpose fully, can cause jealously and often does not lead to harmonious relating. However, when the person who is not fully aligned lets go of any fear he or she has around not being good enough, the division between them and the person who is fulfilling their purpose could instead inspire a mentorship.

As you know, I'm a being who can be quite intimate with you and also be involved with many others as well. I welcome intimate relating and can be available and present for it with countless people at one time. I have allowed my heart to open to its fullest capacity. This is how I can engage with as many people as I do. My heart not only loves to its maximum ability, but it also possesses no one person. In order to engage as I do, to the depths, I have released my need to be exclusively intimate with one being. I agreed to this when asked by the Creators to fulfill the role of being Christed.

In addition to answering your question, my hope for this information being known is that it frees those who want to remain unmarried to do so without judgment. If this is what feels in alignment with their truth, it could mean another type of lifestyle awaits them that they hadn't even considered.

An additional bit of information, in regard to me being available to more than one person at a time, has to do with delegation. Archangels work with me. They form bonds with people. This leads to the angel offering guidance after consulting with me or with the Creators. Knowing one's angel can either further create alignment with one's purpose or can be a challenge for those who feel having a spirit be so close to them is an invasion. I support people in banishing their fear surrounding the latter. Rather, I encourage people to enjoy having this clear guidance and a supportive listener so close at hand. Being judged, of course, is the largest fear surrounding not wanting to know one's angel. Let it be known, however, that there is zero judgment—on any level—coming from me or from the other angels.

Well, that answer solves a huge mystery. Not that I fully comprehend the fact that you are omnipresent, but at least I have something to consider that feels right in my being.

What do you want to know about now, my dear?

This feels like a potentially complicated issue, but it's coming up for me. You're always quoted as using the term "God"—back in the days when you walked the earth in the flesh. Yet, since the beginning of this project, you've used the term "Creators." Would you share more about this?

Back when I walked the earth in the flesh, I was not yet fully aware of who and what sourced the planet. I knew what is now referred to as the "Old Testament" and that the word "God" felt right to me, and I used it as I grew older and began to realize my calling. I also heard spirits and saw angels. All of them let me know I had made a soul agreement with what was called "God" to be Jesus the Christed. I was made aware of the life I was destined to lead, other than the one I already knew. And, in order for the truth known to me to be heard by others, I used the language that was familiar and accepted. Let it be known, dear one, that it was not until I had accepted my death as a man, and moved fully back into my spirit, that I remembered the word "Creators" is most accurate when speaking of both whom and what sourced the planet and its inhabitants.

The term "God" need not be abandoned and can be used properly when it means the Source of all that is powerful and in the highest good. However, it's not being properly used when it's referenced as one being of a male gender that is determining all of life's events. Let this be what I leave you with today.

January 11, 2010

Dear one, today I would appreciate the opportunity to share my childhood memories of my mother, father, and siblings. Would this be okay with you?

Absolutely. People, I'm sure, would want to know all that you're willing to share.

Would you be adverse to me only discussing what will assist others in becoming closer to who they are meant to be, as opposed to me solely sharing tales of my youth?

This is your project. I'm here as your messenger. I'm fine with what you're proposing.

Thank you for your availability to hear my voice. I will begin then. Most of the time, in my youth in Nazareth, it took strength in my body to walk all the places I needed and wanted to go. It was also a time when strength in my mind started to be required. I began reading our sacred scriptures, and believing in certain passages in particular. I would sit in the middle of our village, and those who heard me freely sharing my interpretations of these passages would find spots to sit and be with me. Almost every day, I would stay out from the early hours through the afternoon, talking to all those who seemed quite unhappy. It was at age thirteen when people older than me began looking to me for answers to large questions. One day I realized I was supposed to be doing exactly this, only with many more people.

As I grew older, my mother, father, and I grew very close. We shared our love for one another quite freely. My friends were adopted brothers and sisters, whose original families had died or could no longer tend to them. Caring between us came so easily. I share all this so that you can know just how hard it was to have to leave, in order to spread truth and help others heal. For I was working with healing in ways that, at the time, no one else living in a physical body could do.

It was my devotion to the Creators that fueled my ability to let go of a comfortable home life. I urge anyone who feels similarly about his or her place in the world to not be held back by any obligatory feelings about staying near to family and/or childhood friends. Devotion to one's loved ones is not illustrated by not leaving one's home. It is in this devotional relationship that many people confuse possession for love. Devotion brings with it no commitment of place, but sole commitment of one's heart.

Let it be known that the joy that can be experienced when one has let go of their original home, in order to serve their calling, can be felt by all the person's loved ones—no matter how far apart they may be in miles. I am encouraging all daughters and sons of heaven on earth to, with force, become whoever they are called to be. For it is in this type of action that a healed world can occur once again.

Are you alright, dear one? Are you in need of your own expression at this time?

No, thank you. I'm not in need. I'm rather enjoying your flow.

I'll then continue with another childhood memory. In Nazareth, many trees often tried to communicate with me. One day, I discovered one that offered its name. She and I became friendly after that. From time to time, I would go up to her with some friends, bring lunch, and have a casual conversation. Many other children became curious about her. They would follow whenever I headed there. However one day, upon their arrival, I sensed her becoming concerned and, within a very short amount of time, I was no longer able to hear her voice or feel her branches move.

I decided to no longer allow the other children to go with me when I visited her. I had to go alone many times before I sensed her again. One day, she spoke to me and told me why she left to be only in her spirit instead of being in both her spirit and in the physical tree. She explained that no one I had allowed to come see and speak with her had cared for her in the same way that I did. Her knowing (her intuitive ability within) sensed this, and she didn't want to share herself with anyone who did not care about her.

I continued to visit my friend for years to come and I always went alone. When it came time for me to leave the life I knew and to serve the Creators, I took the very valuable lesson I had received from the tree with me. I learned to care about everyone, despite what they said out of fear that could have otherwise offended me and kept me away.

For I never wanted anyone to feel uncared for in my presence. I always made sure that anyone who truly was in need never felt more in need upon meeting me. I also made sure that anyone who was sad and feeling lonely did not feel a deeper sadness and aloneness after having made my acquaintance. When possible, the people who crossed my path were offered relief to what ailed them—through me.

Let it be known that now is the time for sisterly and brotherly love to pervade the planet. Anything less than this will continue to chip away, not only at Mother Earth's surface, but also at the solitary lives of more people than most realize exist. I hope that anyone who has suffered pain due to another will free themselves from the unsupportive pressure on their heart—so that they will feel true camaraderie for their global family, community, closest loved ones, and themselves.

One can be served tremendously by trusting in the perfect unfolding of why certain painful experiences have come into one's life. For everything occurs to strengthen one's soul for its present life's purpose and its future incarnation. When adopting this belief, letting go of past hurtful memories becomes a lot more easeful.

I know that forgiveness is quite hard to do, and to feel authentically. However, the lack of it keeps much of your planet's darkness alive. And the children of heaven on earth ought to feel heaven on earth. For it has been such a long, long time since this has been one's overall experience.

January 13, 2010

This day I would like to offer some understanding in regard to what was, and is, a most horrific event. I'm speaking of the World War II Holocaust, the killing of millions of people, with over six million of them being Jewish people.

Though many prayed, they did not hear my words, nor did they allow themselves to trust their own intuitive guidance. The Germans were urged by me to not partake in the cruel punishing behavior being asked of them as Nazis. As with many Jewish people, they too did not heed their instincts to leave their homes with their first knowing—within themselves. My life during this time had no peace. Every moment I agonized over what all the children of creation were experiencing.

My heart's energy spread far across Germany, Poland, Belgium, and throughout the rest of Europe. My heart knew many people's torment through that time, those of varied religions, ancestral heritage, age, persuasion, and beliefs.

My role could only be that of consoler for some of these victims being taken from their homes and transported to what would become their darkest nightmare coming true.

Let it be known that not knowing how to stop what was taking place is an important detail of the German culture, and most other cultures are not aware of this. The fact that many countries did not know what was happening is another reason why so many were killed.

Many attempts for "salvation" by holy wars have been made since, as well as prior, to this war. Please let it be known, once and for all, that nothing is further from heaven on earth than slaughtering one another in the name of God, purity, or peace. Nothing!

Whatever you do to one another is also done to all of earth's creatures—no matter how large or small in size. Everything knows when love flows around it safely, and when hate surrounds it as well.

I will end by stating that ethics are incredibly important. They directly affect one's well-being, life circumstances, ability to align with their purpose, and the ability to return to one's soul's mission—lifetime after lifetime. I encourage learning how to discern what is, and is not, for the highest good. By aligning with one's own spirit, one will always know.

I've been anticipating you addressing this topic. I was hoping to have some of my intense feelings about it assuaged. Back in college, I was obsessed with it. I did a research paper on it for a political science class, likening it to the genocides in Bosnia at the time. I watched documentaries consisting of actual footage of Hitler and his troops, as well as interviews with survivors. I believe it was these survivors that were my first exposure to this Holocaust.

I have a memory of my father and me in Manhattan, in a department store elevator, when I was quite young. He subtly pointed to a woman's arm that had a number tattooed on it. As we exited, he told me a little bit about why the number was there and that she was a survivor of the Holocaust. It stayed with me.

It was a while after college, but I made it to Germany during a solo European journey. I needed to see if I could feel some semblance of peace with the people, after losing some of my own people at their hands. I belong to an international host and travelers organization and had profiles of people who opened their homes in Munich. I chose a woman around my age who lived alone. I found her to be very generous with me. I actually felt a kinship. During our time together, she shared her remorse for what had happened in her country—as well as right in her city. She said many people felt a lot of guilt and did not know how to make up for what had happened—confirming what you said.

She let me stay as long as I wanted. This gave me time to explore, have some down time and also visit the closest and first concentration camp: Dachau. It was something I knew I had to do. It was frightful. It reeked of hate and death, but also of hope: hope that never got to see the light of day. Anyway, I don't want to go into all that pain.

I'm wondering if you could shed some light on what caused the Holocaust, at its root?

I can. And yet, first I would like to acknowledge your experience. I know it had been quite difficult having lost family members, and still continuing your journey to the camp. It challenged you greatly. I'm glad you knew your own ability of strength in darkness.

Now I'll speak about the cause. I'll begin by saying that such acts of barbarism can only come from the cruel treatment that also occurred to those who perpetrate it. And hence, you can witness the cycle. Who, or what, began life's first despicable act is the one and only dark force known. There are some who give it a name. However, no name would be accurate. I'm not going to use "evil" or "devil" as words I advocate believing in. I will, however, let my experience of this dark force be known.

A long time ago, approaching my thirty-third year on earth as a man made of flesh, I met up with darkness. I was alone on a mission to hear what, at the time, I called "God." I was determined to hear as clearly as possible. In order to do so, I removed myself from the land to which I had become accustomed. At times, I heard voices on this journey that did not sound loving, peaceful, or guiding. They alarmed my whole being. For these unfamiliar voices were sounds of this darkness. The quality of my character was being tried. Impurities were being forced out. The tiniest residual deformities of my heart were leaving me, due to the visit with darkness.

What happened with Adolph Hitler was a failed attempt by his spirit to utilize the visiting of darkness as an opportunity to further clear out his own darkness. Instead of growing more into who he was meant to be, which was a powerful military peace officer, his spirit allowed the darkness to influence him and to have it become his way of being. We have all seen this occur, to a lesser degree, with others as well.

Dear one, I yearned to have been able to prevent this somehow. I truly mourn, to this day, all the lives that were lost in this genocide—and in countless others. Please be aware that one day all of the Creators' children will know themselves, as well as one another, as who they truly are: God and Goddess, Spirit, Divine Energy—Light.

January 14, 2010

I want to talk today about humans and their desire for power. Although we've discussed the topic, I want to develop it more. Let it be known how expansive one's own power is meant to be. Since time began, all species of all sizes have been evolving in order to explore their complete capabilities. My role now is to inform you that much of the technology created within the last forty years, although it serves society, to a large degree distracts people from their own power. I'm speaking especially of those things that have dramatically changed communication.

Many of the people who are meant to be expanding themselves for the good of all, are not—due to the accessibility of one another through cell phones, and the use of satellites that offer remote viewing of other countries, people, and events. Most assuredly, global technology is the reason. Human-inspired objects are to merely be supplementary devices, but they are receiving the kind of attention that is for destined creations. Therefore, these human-inspired objects are not only a distraction for a person, but the planet is in danger of not acquiring highly important and destined creations.

Let us remember that not only does each and every human being have a destined purpose, some have a role planned for them to create hugely expansive projects. This could come in various forms: from starting a new belief system that helps many people, to going across the planet to capture brilliant photos, stories, or medicines that would also serve others. There are many awaited destined projects, with expansiveness of self and others at their core.

If people's power continues being used to make more and more distractions for themselves and others, your planet will become darker. This will be due to the unhappiness known to each and every person who is not experiencing his or her own power, but rather experiencing the depletion of it. People need to familiarize themselves with their own true power. This is a way to end what is happening.

I know people who are quite able in a few areas. They enjoy dabbling in each. They also share a common complaint, which I had at one time. It's that they feel scattered and don't know what they are truly meant to be doing. Would you talk about how individuals can discern their particular power, or even distinguish their true power from multiple abilities and interests?

Ah, I have heard this cry of concern more times than you would imagine possible! It is that "complaint" that can lead a person to their power, by letting go of all that is not supposed to occur either at this time or during this lifetime. We spoke about darkness just yesterday. Complaining is a form of this energy coming to visit. It can act as an impetus to propel a person into his or her destined role—the role in which they would be most content during this particular lifetime, despite whatever other interests they may have. A person needs to find out the reason for living in their present incarnation, in order to know who they are meant to be—for themselves and for others. Everyone can, and ought to, learn of this particular power that they possess.

Meditation can offer the space to hear what is inside, and what is true for oneself. An additional way to hear is prayerful silence—to sit quietly, with the intention of hearing one's own heart and/or spirit guides and listening for an answer to the question at hand. An important consideration with prayerful silence is about what form the answer will take. Having an open mind allows one's answers to be recognized and received.

Answers generally come in a variety of ways despite one's usual method of seeing them. An example is hearing someone unrelated to one's life talking about the issue with which one is dealing. Knowing that the information is meant for you, the questioner, is what is important.

Learning to understand the answers is also critical. One does not necessarily lead to the other. In other words, when one is guided to go or be somewhere, it may not be due to positive happenings that will induce gratification. But most assuredly, an answer is awaiting that person's understanding. It may sound game-like, and in a way it is. However, each and every step to a person's true power has been considered by his or her guides. These guides know intimately with whom they are working. This makes all of the steps perfect.

Despite these perfect steps being available, they're

often not followed. Yet, even one's own way of arriving into their power can offer such a profound spiritual education. When the arriving occurs in more lives, you and I will see more world-expanding creations.

Dear one, a long time ago, when I was an able carpenter, all the villagers adored my detailed woodwork. There were those who traveled far to purchase pieces of furniture that my mother's husband and I built together. For some time, this is what I pictured as my livelihood—my lifestyle. However, I couldn't let go of my dream of sharing the truth about how life was meant to be lived. I wanted to share with whoever had the ears to hear, the heart to know, and the recognition of loving compassion. I came to see this as an important road for me to be walking, and the only road for me to follow. Despite how respected and appreciated I was for my carpentry, teaching was more a part of me. Teaching had to be chosen, in order for me to receive the power awaiting me. By doing so, I became powerful enough to give more and more.

I feel that it's time to end this topic for today. My hope is that everyone from this day forward will find his or her most powerful role to live in this lifetime.

I hope so too. What a planet it would be if this were the case. One day . . . .

Now, I'm incredibly curious about why you referred to Joseph as your "mother's husband." Would you quickly comment on this before we close today? As I'm writing, I realize we haven't spoken about him before—so please . . . .

I don't want to begin another important conversation this afternoon. I promise that the next time we talk, I'll

begin with Joseph. Thank you, dear one, for your patience
and ability to hear what is meant to be heard.

You're welcome. And I understand. I'm a bit tired, and yet I
didn't want to wait until next time to acknowledge what seemed
significant.

Ah, until next time, dear sister.

January 15, 2010

⟨≈⟩

I'm here with you now, back from supporting many souls in repairing their loving hearts—hearts they thought were broken beyond repair. Do you still want to know about Joseph, dear one?

It's nice to hear what you've been doing the last twenty hours. You usually don't share that with me. And yes, I'd like to know about Joseph.

I welcome everyone who has ears to hear, and a heart that is presently willing to learn about Joseph—my beloved soul father. Our Mother Mary did not conceive me from Joseph's DNA. However, Joseph's energy brought me up to believe in who I was then, and who I am now. It was his loving role modeling that assisted me in knowing what a man ought to be. This significantly impacted all of my interactions with other males, and most particularly in the way I related with females. Joseph offered me such depth of love, for which I am grateful beyond measure.

I ask men today to consider Joseph's modeling in regard to keeping one's word. He never said anything he didn't mean. And for all of the town's children, this was significant. The majority of the other fathers did not follow through with many statements they made. Joseph also respected older people. He illustrated this whenever he and I would go into town together. He allowed the elders to walk slowly in front of him without asking them to step aside or stop, so that he could hurry past. Joseph would remain at a distance instead, so they would not feel crowded or nervous. My hope is that Joseph's spirit will be called forth by anyone—man or woman, child or young adult—in order to learn how to respect and honor one's self and others.

My time with Joseph also lent itself to me not allowing what others said about me to affect me in a negative manner. For it was all the loving guidance given through him, straight to me, that taught me forgiveness. During my time in human form, I experienced many people's hate and judgment toward me. So this ability to forgive served me well when I was both hanging on the cross and living by it, while walking on the earth. Coming to an understanding of Joseph's words about having mercy and releasing anger is what saved my spirit.

Thank you for speaking openly. It's such a beautiful relationship to know about. It's also quite illuminating. I had no idea how influential Joseph was in your life. I guess this is because much of the years we've spent together in communication, you've been listening to me. And so now I'm incredibly curious:

If Joseph was not your biological father, then who was? Indeed, it's hard to even ask this question, because it feels enormous.

It's no more enormous than any of the other disclosures about which we've conversed. And I don't have a biological father! A star seed was planted inside Mary's uterus when she was brought into the world. My fetal self was set to come into being when she became mature enough to give birth and to care for me.

Are you confirming the immaculate conception theory?

No, I am not confirming that Mary and Joseph didn't have sexual intercourse and that I was born through one God's life force. What I am confirming is that, whether or not Mary chose to marry Joseph, or remain single, I still would have been birthed through her. Conceiving in the traditional way was not required for me to be born. For I was destined to arrive as Yeshua—Jesus— despite Mary's choice to become active sexually or to have been celibate. Let it be known this was not and still isn't the situation for any other star seed births. For only my birth had to occur no matter what!

Let me speak now about star seeds. They are light forms made from the Creators' as well as from the sun's energy. Deliberateness behind a star seed is what creates so much power within each one. For example, Mother Theresa was also a star seed planted in her mother's uterus when her mother was just ready to enter the earth. As you have already learned, Mother Theresa was the reincarnation of Mother Mary. This was possible due to Mary's angelic nature. A deliberate understanding of purpose had to be established before the Creators would agree to her reincarnation. When this became clear, and known as significant in its intention, Mary's light was turned into a planted star seed.

Multiple saints now living on your planet were born of star seeds. As with Mary, only angelic beings are able to reincarnate as saints. This is one who offers his or her whole being for the highest good of everyone and everything. Let it be known how blessed you and your soul sisters and brothers are to learn from, and be able to model, these individuals. For it is our hope that you all will be able to recognize yourselves, through their existence on earth.

It's now okay for you to ask how you can identify these people. I hear you wanting to know who they are.

Yes, you're hearing my unspoken thoughts. I have some ideas about who these saints are. Also, I have an understanding of how it feels to be around such a being—by experiencing you, and most recently Mary. If you deem it in the highest good to disclose the identities of these people, I, and I imagine others, would be glad to hear. I leave it completely up to you.

I will inform you of some, and let you figure out the others. Thich Nhat Hanh, your present Dalai Lama, Henry David Thoreau, and Martin Luther King Jr. were all star seeds. All were once angels who became saints. These beings made their agreements after clarifying a deliberate purpose for returning. All of them walked your planet before their present, or most recent, lifetime took place. All of them also knew huge changes needed to happen in order to move society ahead spiritually. Each one has now accomplished their destined purpose.

Now, dear one, all that I've just shared with you has been a bit shocking to your system. I think it's time to let this information settle, and to reconvene after the week-end respite. Would this be alright with you? For it truly feels right to me.

Your perception is accurate. I feel affected, blown open, actually, by the depth of your sharing, so I agree to close for today. Please know my heart is more full of you, after hearing the intimate details about your life. I'm so glad we will meet again during these conversations. Alas, I bid you adieu . . . .

January 18, 2010

Today I hear your unspoken thoughts again. You need a better understanding as to why Jewish people have been judged and persecuted. I know wherever there is one person who doesn't fully understand something, there are usually many more. So I looked into the hearts of the other Jewish people, who also don't fully understand anti-Semitism, and this made things clear to me.

It's that some people believe the Jews caused my death. And there are some who use Judas' religious belief system as an excuse to persecute an entire race. This, however, is nothing other than mass disobedience to one's self and to one's brothers, sisters, and planet. This includes telling lies of "convenience," to making "small" remarks that are filled with judgment and speak hate, to attempts to clear a group of people from the human family.

My experience of this is horrific. For any time one person persecutes another, I feel it. Let it be known in the hearts of all people, that my death was caused by the Creators so that I could align with my purpose—to be reborn into the spirit realm and to continue my work more pervasively!

Thank you for addressing what was on my mind, and in my heart. I feel good about what you said. What did you want to share prior to connecting with me?

My original thought for today was to have us talk about allowing one's own personality to come through, once one has aligned with his or her soul's purpose. It's important to hold on to that which supports one's essence. It is, however, equally as important to let go of all that's no longer supportive.

When I was younger, as I have shared before, I knew I was born to be a teacher of the truths that I heard come through me from the Creators. What I didn't share, however, was how I also enjoyed being lazy and not doing anything at all. I experienced much pleasure in staying awake late into the night—talking, drinking, and flirting with women. I let myself enjoy this for one year's time. I then knew I had to make a choice between the two lives I had been living. Although it was uncomfortable to let go of all that seemed to be rightfully mine to experience, the call to align with my purpose was louder. It did take a bit of time to fully accept going without what I had been accustomed to having, and to realize that what was once comfortable was no longer supportive. Clinging to unsupportive personality traits inhibits one's ability to fully align with his or her purpose. Not allowing such traits to fall away is to go against one's truest intention for oneself.

Autumn always turns to winter. Spring always turns to summer. Each season changes into the next without holding on to what it must leave behind. And so it is for the earth's people as well. When it comes time to evolve through one's chrysalis, to birth the wings of a butterfly, in order for the natural course of life to continue moving forward, one ought not resist.

Dear one, would you discuss what you have allowed to fall away, in order to align with your purpose? Whatever you are comfortable sharing, I would find helpful as examples.

As soon as you asked me, I saw the list begin to compile in my head: Analyzing, talking about others, certain relationships and beliefs, excess sugar and caffeine (and the foods and beverages containing them), and the list goes on. However, some of the things I allowed to fall away were ripe enough that I didn't experience much discomfort with letting them go. Worrying, however, is one thing that I'm presently trying to let fall away. I learned from you that it isn't supportive and that I needed to replace it with trusting my own knowing.

It's not that I needed to hear that it wasn't supportive; I could sense that myself. Yet, my own acknowledgement wasn't enough to stop it. I've had to really be with it, to see how many things there are with which I haven't felt at ease. Working with my guides, and being committed to being aligned with my spirit, has diminished my hold on worrying. I see how this behavior dissipates my energy. I also see how it doesn't support who I've realized I am.

I know how many external pleasures you've allowed to fall away once you began to realign with your purpose. I've watched you let go of all the previously mentioned behaviors—despite your urges, cravings, and desire. This was a lengthy clearing process. You have faltered at times. And so it will be the same with worry. However, you now retrieve your ease and peace at a much quicker pace.

Let it be known that everyone can also allow faltering to occur when true commitment to one's own evolution exists. It can be the misstep that brings one even closer to the heart of his or her alignment. For it is most important to remember that darkness is meant to assist one in going deeper into whom they are intended to be. It also has the ability to propel one out of their alignment indefinitely. I encourage all people to resist this, and only this.

January 21, 2010

Today, let us acknowledge that these are war times. I ask that anyone who is a war veteran or presently active call on my heart, in order for his or her spirit to be cared for in the midst of any trauma or grief.

My work includes offering solace to those whose loved ones have gone off to fight a war that they shouldn't need to fight. A soldier's courage ought not be forgotten or dishonored. However, it still remains that war, as it is now fought in the world, goes against the divine nature of how heaven on earth is intended to be experienced. I listen to all of the soldiers' hearts on your planet on a regular basis. Please know how much fear and pain these people are carrying with them—not only when they enter into battle, but almost every moment.

A new way of handling disagreements needs to be established. Not only those involved in war directly are in danger, but your entire planet is in danger of losing morale, peace, and joy amongst the rest of the human race. Fear and despair already pervade the hearts of people throughout the many countries. Americans, although generous toward other countries, also remain insulated. This is not the fault of any specific individuals, and is rather caused primarily by their fear of getting too involved where they may not be welcome.

My experience has shown me that the desire in the hearts of many Americans is to serve as volunteers in a foreign country—both in and out of their field of expertise. Prejudice against Americans has developed, due to actions conducted by prior heads of state. This has left those who yearn to offer themselves to various parts of the globe feeling unsafe to do so. It is vital that each and every person be heard and known for who they are, rather than being assumed to uphold a similar belief system and ethic as those who run (or have run) their country of origin.

Darkness needn't be seen in everyone, when it's only a few who don't clearly know what's honorable and for the highest good. As all on your planet have witnessed, others who have previously judged whole nations according to the choices of a few have caused much harm.

January 22, 2010

Today I would like to share more about the hopes I possess for those who will be reading these words. Although I don't appear humble at times, be aware that I'm feeling no judgment—only humility—toward all the people on the earth. This isn't due to any hidden grandiosity on my part, and neither is it because I don't believe in my experience. Rather, it's due to all the beautiful creations developed for the betterment of the people and the planet.

I am in awe of the buildings that are intricate in their architecture, and the cities cradling them, all with accessibility and existing to be enjoyed. And I am in awe of the jewelry—polished, carved, made by digging into the planet's core—adorning people in many cultures, at times in order to honor beginning a new life with a beloved. And I am in awe of the colors made from vegetables and used to dye fabrics for clothing and homes.

My heart opens wide when it is exposed to so much

elegant beauty. However, beauty runs deeper than the external form. Watching all the people who need food being fed via an established soup kitchen, and seeing that they have a place to receive care via shelters, blows my heart completely open. My hope is that one will enjoy elegant beauty, as well as beauty that is not so elegant. For there are more people who won't be warm and fed tonight than those who will. There are those who are without money, due to a tragedy they experienced, and there are those in need—not due to a specific event but to darkness overtaking their spirit.

Let it be known that there is enough money in your societies to clothe, house, and feed all those in existence. I ask that more thought, combined with Christ-like action, be directed toward those who don't have enough. And I ask that one sees this as beautiful, and as a way of honoring others and themselves. Dear one, would you share your experience with this? I know that you've had various attitudes during your journey.

My ten years in New York City offered me the opportunity to evolve, with regard to this topic. Initially, I had judgment about the homeless—and people asking for money in general. Most of the acquaintances I made early on ignored these folks, as we saw them on the streets every day. The general opinion was that the homeless people would "only use the money for alcohol and drugs," and therefore it wasn't a good idea to give any away. I saw myself continuing to further shut down around these people—even when I was alone. I wouldn't look at them or acknowledge their requests.

After some time, I stopped meeting with the aforementioned acquaintances. And I began seeing a man who later became my partner for a number of years. One of the acts he did altered my perspective profoundly. We were approached by someone in need, and my partner's response was to walk to the nearby market and buy this man groceries. When the bag was handed over to him, everything in me shifted.

It was hard for me to acknowledge that, at the time, because I didn't feel cared for in a deep or sensitive way by my partner. However, the experience stayed with me and became a model. Toward the end of our relationship, my Buddhism studies began. These teachings helped facilitate me seeing all beings as equally important. I started looking in the eyes of every person and creature I encountered, in order to cultivate and develop a sense of equanimity. I presently go out of my way to let someone know I see them with gratitude, despite their circumstances and including their circumstances!

I'm now remembering my recent time in India. There was so much need, and lack of equanimity. It was difficult for me to be around it, and I wondered how the wealthy were able to witness all that and not assist. I imagine some did. Yet, the conditions were so extreme in their opposition that it was difficult to know if anyone was taking steps to even it out. Jesus, would you shed a little light on how this inequity can exist in the world?

Dear one, first I want to acknowledge your intimate expression. It's appreciated. Now, I'll answer your question. Many people don't know that all other people are the sons and daughters of the Creators. They most likely don't know that they are also sons and daughters of the same Creators. This non-acknowledgment of the true nature of things keeps societies from growing together with equanimity. Hence, extreme differences occur in social and financial status. However, no actual difference exists internally—spiritually.

And yet, there are differences in one's evolutionary timing. It is quite different for everyone. This ought to be known, and considered. For one's stage of evolution determines the depth of one's feelings and abilities in all experiences.

January 25, 2010

Today, I would like to share something deeply personal. I'm sharing it because I hope those who learn about it will be inspired. For it's through honest and intimate disclosure of one's struggles that real relating happens.

During my lifetime on earth, many people asked to assist me during my varied jobs. They wanted to help with carpentry projects and with clearing landscapes for planting. However, I only accepted help from one person and was then later accused of having relations with her unrelated to the work we were doing. I was concerned for her reputation as well as mine, so I ended our working relationship. Her heart then fractured and her sweet temperament soured.

In confidence, I had told her all my stories of growing up and knowing I was meant to help others evolve. When I let her know we could no longer work together, she spread these stories around to unfriendly hearts. I felt quite alone, betrayed, and hurt. Despite these feelings, however, I continued on the path I knew was intended for me. It took time to reestablish my ability to trust others. But I chose to not allow that experience to poison the trust I could have in new friendships. It didn't take long before these relationships proved themselves worthy of engaging in—even more fully than the one in which I had been betrayed.

As it turned out, the hurt I had experienced assisted in my personal growth and my ability to relate with others in ways that felt more meaningful. A deeper and more compassionate way of being had developed in me. I learned to value intimate disclosure of painful experiences—for, when I shared mine, it freed others to do so as well.

My hope is that people will begin sharing their hurts in order to allow compassion to be born in their relationships. When more people in your society begin being real with one another, a whole new experience of life will occur. All the hiding lends itself to acting out harshly either toward someone else or toward oneself. Often, it's both. The only time anyone ought not speak about what is real for them is when, intuitively, the person knows that their listener cannot understand them. For example, when a two-year-old spills her breakfast and the child's parent is overwhelmed and distraught (due to the piles of bills or an absent partner), the child shouldn't be burdened with his or her parent's challenges.

I'm not suggesting that people should talk directly with strangers about what is real for them. (However, at times, this could be exactly what is in the highest good.) I am suggesting that the boldness with which people share vivid details that don't help one another evolve be transferred to vivid, real interpersonal exchanges.

The details to which I refer are the private matters of others. Someone's business, when it's requested to be kept private, ought not become public. Although the person publicly sharing the private information may believe that a level of intimate expression is being experienced. In actuality, no one receives anything other than the feeling of being disheartened.

I'm conscious of the fact that engaging in what is considered "gossip" has a high value placed on it—both in the media's financial dependence on it, and in its long history as an accepted tradition. My interest lies in dispelling the belief that any goodness can come from the stories of someone, other than one's self, being told publicly without permission. One's time is better used to focus on the capacity to feel self-acceptance and to eliminate doubt regarding one's own worthiness.

Dear one, I'm honored to witness your growing acceptance of both yourself and others. Please discuss a bit about how this relates to learning to not talk about people. However, it's not necessary to do this today. Rather, maybe tomorrow or when you and I next come together to discuss global considerations. For now I must go.

January 27, 2010

Good afternoon. Is there anything pressing, or are you fine
with beginning where we left off?

Hello there. No, nothing feels pressing. I can go ahead and
share my experience with learning to not gossip about people.
At one time, it seemed right to talk about others. Back in high
school, all my friends talked about each other. I don't feel good
about this. I wish I would've known better.

Thinking about it, I see now that it has a direct line to fear
and jealousy. And both these words probably point to the feeling of not being worthy. As I aged into my twenties, I continued
talking about others. Again, everyone seemed to do so, without questioning if it was right. Within the last few years, it has
become known to me, in my body, that it's not something in
which I wish to participate. And if I do it, even in the smallest
of ways, it feels wounding to myself and to the person about
whom I've spoken.

I now know I am divine energy having a human life (at least

most of the time), and I understand that discussing someone in the way we have described isn't compatible with this identity. Knowing who I am also allows me to understand that others are divine energy as well. This too keeps me from wanting to talk about them. Not gossiping has helped me to like and accept myself more. And it does take effort. To me, it's like not reaching for things I'm drawn to simply for instant gratification. These things ultimately leave me feeling as toxic as they are.

Your journey to end your relationship with speaking behind people's backs may have taken you into your thirties. However, you have arrived.

I would like to now move on and talk about the time when I traveled to India. I know many people don't realize I went, both now and in my lifetime in my physical body. However, the time there impacted me and is worth discussing. There I received meditation training, dharma studies, and learned the skill of not talking all the time—to rather listen to the hearts of others as well as to my own.

The hours I spent at the monastery where I studied offered me an appreciation for Buddhism that is tremendous. However, many who follow this religion don't believe in the Creators as I know them. Despite this difference, my gratitude goes out to Buddha Shakyamuni who started this devotional way of learning to care for one's self and others. The time has come for all of creation to care for each other with such devotion.

My hope is for all religions to release their attachment to believing only their doctrine, and to become open to creation coming through divine energy of no specific denomination.

Let it be known that this divine energy also exhibits no

specific image. God is thought to be a white male. Generally, those who believe that I'm God depict me as being
white and occasionally as African-American. However God,
otherwise known as Source and Creation, is not white or
African-American. And at this point, I have no race. A long
time ago, as a man in my thirties, my hair was brown and
it came down to my shoulders. I was lean and wore cot-
ton cloth cinched at the waist with a thin leather strap. At
times, I had facial hair and other times I didn't. But now, this
body I describe is no longer part of who I am and I instead
exist as a high vibration white light. However, when I want
individuals to know I am with them, I appear in a way that
assists them in relating to me. For some people, I show up
as a white man with brown hair. For others, I show up as
an African-American man, and it's the way of all the other
angels as well.

Dear one, this is what I want everyone to know and
understand. My soul will always be the same, no matter
how the person looks who wants to communicate with
me. My desire is for unity among nations to abound, and
for those who know me to believe in the truth I share. And
at the moment, this truth comes directly through a daughter of Creation who hears my heart as clearly as she hears
her own.

No pressure there . . . I tend to believe I hear your heart
more clearly than mine. But I sense it's time to truly hear what
you're saying about me and trust it. Not to digress, but you did
tell me this morning that it's time to know that I *know*, and to
consult with you less. So, thank you for the confirmation here
during this conversation.

I'm intrigued and thrilled by what you shared today. It feels like a common thread can be sewn through many people's belief systems now. At least let's hope! A question that comes from listening to you is this: Why are there then so many races, with the countless varieties of human beings serving as a catalyst for wars?

Of course you know you'll have to await the answer with bated breath . . . ha, ha, ha! For now, you and I have other tasks to work on. Namaste.

January 28, 2010

Today I'm going to answer your most recent question. I'm going to talk about the variety of beautiful faces, hair types, and colors that our Creators have designed for people. Colors, textures, and other details add flavor, dimension, and enjoyment when one cooks or creates any work of art. This is also the case when it comes to why there are so many races in existence. Each culture plays a vital role in what is intended to be an awesome array of possibilities for learning—not insurmountable challenges.

Whatever challenges ensue, let it be known that racial wars began during the time of King Solomon. For he did not fully understand what "God" wanted for the sons and daughters of Israel. Many Jews and Gentiles were told that nothing positive could develop from knowing one another, other than through business endeavors. All but a few regarded his words as truthful. It was then that racial prejudice began. It was as if those who had it in them suddenly felt free to release and express it to their neighbors.

My understanding of how this occurred didn't come to me until I became spirit, after being freed from my flesh. And yet, I sensed King Solomon's lack of clarity in hearing "God's" wishes as early as my childhood—while listening to Jewish scriptures. I heard messages, parables, and prophecies. Some of these felt comforting, but I experienced many as being wrongly understood—not only by others who heard the same words as I did, but also by those who originally heard them and transcribed them as the words of "God. " I knew God was kinder and more loving than portrayed.

Now that I've described this background, let's not forget how far many humans have gone in disregard and disrespect towards those who are foreign to them. I excuse anyone who has never judged another person for looking or acting differently than himself or herself. However, nearly one hundred percent of the earth's population doesn't know what it's like to never have been made to feel ashamed of their religion, race, or culture. There have been too many who have been judged, ridiculed, or dishonored for how they have been perfectly placed on the earth!

Prejudice is caused by fear. It's not something that's learned by listening to one's spirit guides or to one's heart. Doctrine, when followed, no matter who is reading it or critiquing it, is meant to be evaluated and discerned for truth by each individual. Each person should decide whether or not a teaching is true for him or her. Seeing people do this has been a rare occasion. However, when someone does, the whole population knows of it.

My hope for today lies in people now understanding

why they don't look like their neighbors—and in people letting go of centuries of hate due to misunderstanding. My intention is to illuminate how one wrongly informed person in authority can, and has, led many people into hating one another. And for it to be known that it's not only the one who leads who is responsible, but also those who follow without listening to what their intuition is telling them.

It took King Solomon years of hearing what he continued to call "God" before he truly heard accurately. During which, he traveled back to earth and incarnated as different religious figures each time. He was a pope, a catholic priest, a Jewish Kabbalah scholar, and a Native American shaman. Only then did he learn to truly hear the Creators.

Solomon now remains in the spirit realm as high vibration white light. He only guides those who once knew him, before he learned to accurately hear the Creators. All those who had received incorrect guidance are now offered the truth. The degree to which anyone hears Solomon's truths has solely to do with his or her wanting to truly know them.

This was such a difficult session for me. I didn't feel comfortable when you began, and even as you continued. Ironically enough, now I see the parallel with today's topic. I was worried about hearing incorrectly what you were saying about Solomon. So much felt on the line regarding his character's integrity, as well as the potential judgment for the Jews.

I'm glad to see where you've landed with it. There seems to be somewhat of a peaceful resolve. However, I'm still uncomfortable about the lineage of racial disharmony being linked to Israel.

I'm not accusing the Jewish people of beginning racial disharmony! I'm only clarifying one of the oldest questions in existence. Regardless of King Solomon's religious persuasion, his authority—combined with his ability to hear and decipher truth—has everything to do with the origin of racial disharmony. This information is meant to be known to help uncover improper use of power by some of those in charge—and to illustrate how one's disregard of his or her own knowing can also end up culminating in racial, or any other kind of, disharmony. Dear child, you are not obliged to put anything in our manuscript that you don't want to make public. I trust your intuition.

January 30, 2010

~~~~~~~

I'm aware how our most recent conversation felt uncomfortable to you. However, regarding its content, I do consider it to be important. I previously said, and still believe, that you are the one who has the final decision about what appears in the manuscript and what doesn't. However, my hope is that you won't take it out. For it's in no way incriminating against my beloved brothers and sisters of Israel, but rather a necessary illumination of each person's need to be quite clear about whom they follow. One must know, in their heart and intuitively, that they believe in a person before they offer a gift that is as important as their trust!

I'm now going to speak about a time long ago, when my spirit wanted someone or something to believe in. My search went on until darkness found me and tested my ability to stand up to it. At first, I didn't know how. I then learned by remaining still and quiet in the presence of this darkness.

My reason for sharing this has to do with one of your spirit's challenges. Let it be known that this challenge is pervasive—for you are surely not the only one who struggles with remaining still enough to hear your own heart and your own intuitive knowing, when darkness comes calling.

When darkness appears, others as well as you ought not feel as though you are victims. Nor should you feel as though I, or the Creators, have neglected your desire for peace and joy. For these states derive from one's ability to work through darkness. One receives strength, clarity, and resolution through allowing for stillness and quietness.

As a result, many people awaken to the ways they are conditioned to accept false limitations during times when they are trying to dispel darkness.

Becoming aware of old patterns of learned behavior lets one's own true essence come through, instead of the unwanted reactions toward situational triggers. And getting to know each of these triggers, in order to be able to experience ease in all areas of one's life, is encouraged.

Thank you for encouraging more stillness. I've learned that there is great power in it. Now, I'm rather curious about how "long ago" it was that you were searching for someone or something to believe in. It sounds like a place in the conversation worth revisiting. Is there anything regarding this statement that you want to expand further?

I want to thank you for realizing that what you heard required qualification. The time in history to which I referred was one of my incarnations when I was alone, without anyone other than strangers to call friends. Loneliness had taken over my mind, until one day I couldn't bear it anymore. All I wanted was to feel a moment of peace, but I wasn't able to—due to my inability to accept my wife's death. My heart had closed. And I didn't believe in anything to help me move through what had happened. Having been brought up Jewish, my family of origin believed in one almighty God. Love for this God came easily for them, but not for me.

At the time when I became of age to marry, my wife and I decided to not follow Judaism. Rather, we chose to devote ourselves solely to believing in one another. After her death, I had no one other than myself. My family and I didn't see eye to eye about me letting go of Judaism. Also, her family disliked me for "stealing" her away from their religious way of living. So then, at twenty-one years of age and widowed, I only knew darkness—the kind of darkness caused by alienation from myself and from everyone else.

It wasn't long before I realized that in order to continue living, I had to find peace. One day, I decided to hear the birds sing their songs. My belief in them began to develop. I then decided to hear all the animals signaling love to one another—and to me. My heart started to open to every one of the forest creatures. Many years passed, however, until I was able to ultimately love myself. I learned that, by quieting my mind and becoming still, I was able to know my heart and trust that I was valuable.

Despite this, I had only a few moments of peace per day. My heart was missing what it also needed in order to have a joyful and easeful life: a relationship with another divine being.

Dear one, despite all the time spent on getting to know the songs of birds and so on, I felt alone. For I allowed in no one other than my beloved. I died long before I should have—not due to illness or accident, but by letting go of hope that my life could have been anything other than a place of isolation and grief. My heart called out for my lost love, as I died at the age of forty-one. Now, let it be known that I was never actually alone. However, I resisted allowing spirit guides to enter my life. I only understood life through what I had heard from religious books, not from the songs sung by birds or from my own inner knowing.

Thank you for sharing yet another episode from one of your human lives. It makes me feel more of a resonance with you regarding the human struggles. Sometimes I forget that you've been through all of them. I now better understand your passion and compassion. It comes from you having lived through the challenges of walking through life on earth.

I don't want to forget to quiet down and listen to my heart, and to you, when darkness comes. I'm happy to say that I now forget to do so less and less. But when I do, please be loud in reminding me that the darkness is really a growth opportunity— a chance to experience my power more intimately and to feel its expansion.

I'm on the edge of my chair; my cat insists on sitting with me. We agree that she'll stay behind me so that I don't have to lean over her to write. I feel her body breathing into the small of my back. I feel connected to the breath of all existence at this moment. I realize now that she too can remind me. Goodnight.

February 1, 2010

Dear child of creation, my heart is telling me that you are tired of hearing stories. I'm interested in letting you decide where our conversation will go this day. I don't feel pulled in any specific direction. However, if you don't have a question or topic about which you're curious, let it be known that all you are experiencing in your life can be questioned and discussed. For example, I'm aware that you're not excited about the man with whom you're having dinner tonight. I can offer everything that I believe you would benefit from knowing regarding this. Perhaps it will inspire other important topics.

This isn't what I expected for today. But the last two times we came together, it wasn't what I expected either. And it was vexing for me. I'm sorry to say so, but it's my truth. I imagine that's why you're sensing some resistance within me. I hope I can fulfill your wish and continue to record all that you're wanting people to know. The last couple of sessions caused me some doubt. But having said that, I feel a little better. So, I'm open to your idea. Please share what you'd like, in regard to my evening plans.

I experience so much joy from witnessing your happiness; all the many times you smiled, laughed, or danced from having the feeling of sincere pleasure. In addition to these moments, I have witnessed your painful moments as well. It's because of them that I eagerly encourage you to no longer allow anyone into your intimate life who can't offer you what you need.

All that you've worked toward ought not be forgotten in order to have a night out. I know this man is solely a platonic friend. However, all energy is sacred and is meant to be honored. When you come to know someone with whom you're aware you don't resonate, you would do well to no longer offer your time to this person.

I've seen the two of you together. You require more presence from your friends. He's unable to provide clear deliberate communication in your conversations. Most likely, he won't ever offer this. Let it be known that, in order to receive what one's spirit is seeking, one has to let go of whatever is not serving it.

I'm not suggesting you end all relating with this person. However, I am recommending that you only meet on rare occasion. Neither of you need to expend your precious energy where the highest good is not being experienced.

Authenticity, I'm aware, has tremendous importance in your life. Fearing its general nonexistence, as well as at times not feeling courageous enough to establish it in a relationship of your own, has challenged you. Your constant evaluation of its presence in all your actions, words, and beliefs ought not be forgotten.

As soon as I heard the word "authenticity," I got excited. It is so important to me. And even though it pervades my life, I feel the need to have it in every nook and cranny. When you sense me struggling with it, it most likely goes back to old programming and conditioning—to times when I learned that it wasn't safe to look into someone's eyes and tell them truth that they didn't want to hear. It's still not something I enjoy doing. Yet, the consequences of not doing it are more painful.

Has authenticity remained the same for you, or have your beliefs about it been altered?

I appreciate your question. My relationship with it has definitely shifted over time. My heart, rather than my head, leads the evaluations now. And I don't mean emotions versus rationality, with emotions winning.

The heart, for me, is becoming more of a place of knowing rather than an area of deep emotion. It's been an evolution. No steps were skipped. I've felt my life's traumas and challenges. And now my heart receives more rest than it used to. This way I'm able to hear its evaluations of situations. There is very little rigidity now, when I'm observing whether something is authentic or not. There's room for shades of gray, humanity, and divinity.

For example, although the man you spoke of—the one with whom I have dinner plans—is not someone with whom I feel one hundred percent resonance, I do know him to be a good person who listens the best he can, works on himself in order to be more present, and makes me laugh. Also, I find myself resonating less with both old and new friends. My authentic feeling

is that I don't want to disengage with everyone. So, my response
is to have less contact and to try to enjoy the connections when
they do occur.

Dear one, I am proud that you have reached a place
where you feel authentic; not only with your plan for the
evening, but with your life so far. Tonight will be alright for
you as long as you know who you are, what you need, and
what is and is not acceptable.

February 3, 2010

Dear one, today I would very much enjoy sharing another significant lifetime. Let it also be known that I would not only enjoy hearing you before I share, but I encourage it. We can talk about anything about which you're wondering.

I appreciate your openness. And yet, I feel quenched. I welcome your story!

Then I'll share about the lifetime I had when I learned that love between two people who are meant to be together ought only occur when both people are fully and completely ready to love unselfishly. When I was a young boy of age nine, nobody cared for me. Everyone was so busy preparing for a feared invasion.

Our village was located in the foothills of what you now call Wyoming. Legends of wolves becoming friends to children moved from camp to camp. One day, while traveling on my own through a wooded area, a wolf—one as small as a turtle—crossed my path. I decided to allow it to come home with me. My family asked that she remain quiet, so as to not reveal our hiding place to anyone. Not only did she not let anyone know where we were, she never howled at all. All of the other wolves I'd known before always howled in the evening whenever they felt alone or hungry.

It wasn't long before we needed to travel again. We received word that the invaders would be arriving soon. When the time came to leave, I couldn't locate my wolf. Until then, she had always stayed close. I made a decision to not go until I found her. Night came on the day of departure, and I let my father know how I felt about not leaving Tunkal behind. I asked if he would allow me to stay in order to await her return.

During "Native American" times, a boy of nine was often considered mature enough to remain alone if a situation called for it. My father consented to this being one of those times. All night, I waited for Tunkal to come to me. I longed to see her fur that was the color of red hot embers, and her eyes that were the color courage would look like if one could see it.

That night was the first time a spirit came to me. I was sitting by a fire, by which I'd planned to cook dinner and then sleep beside, when she called me by my name: "Samoqryl." Illuminated, this spirit told me that my wolf had been killed by vultures and was never to be found—for they had devoured her.

My heart had once felt empty and cold. But, due to my relationship with Tunkal, it had become full of love and devotion. Let it be known that, until then, I had never wanted to care for another so deeply.

I stood up and asked my spirit guide not to go away,

but to stay with me. Her eyes filled with love, as she agreed. I sensed and knew her energy from then on. Her presence never surprised me, nor was it unwelcome. Her interest in my well-being appeared to be her sole purpose. Her comfort helped me get through many tough nights to come.

I decided not to follow my parents, but to live on my own for a while. I grew up fast and Kindr, my guide, helped tremendously. Her strong yet tender way allowed me to find out what I needed to know. Just the right amounts of fear and strength developed within myself. My body turned into that of a man's and my hunting skills were sharp. Kindr told me the only thing left that I needed was love in physical form, and that she'd see to it that I met a woman when the time was right.

But I hesitated to allow anyone to know me other than Kindr. I felt at ease when alone with her. For nothing needed qualifying or explanation in order to be understood. My heart found her to be a perfect companion, despite the fact that she wasn't human. Loving her was not only enjoyable, but also satisfying enough.

However, one night around a campfire, her words broke my young heart. Kindr said that we had to part; that our time together had come to an end. My breath began to shorten during each intake of air. I cried for the first time in my life, and I felt as though I'd never stop. Kindr held me until I relaxed and was able to understand her words. She told me that her mission was complete and that she needed to be free to go to her next place to fulfill her destiny. Kindr made me aware that I, too, had a destiny. And, in order for me to fulfill it, we needed to say goodbye.

I only accepted what she told me due to the amount of love I possessed for her. Somehow, I had learned to care enough about her to want her happiness more than my own. Her heart also knew this. When our last night together came, I didn't cry. Rather, my eyes were full of wonder for my own destiny.

The howling wind came through our campsite, her presence began diminishing and then nothing of her remained. My body aged as the wind quieted down. It was not because years had passed but, rather, because her light was gone. It had illuminated my environment, and it also illuminated me. Having her near kept me filled with her light; and with her gone, I began to fill myself.

I met my destiny. About two years later, one evening while I was preparing dinner, a magnificent red-haired woman who went by the name Tunkal entered my campsite. We didn't leave one another's side until death took us.

It was then I saw Kindr again, upon my reentrance into the spirit realm. There she revealed that she was my wife's mother, and I had known her only briefly—right before I was to incarnate as Samoqryl.

She also made me aware that she had asked me to care for her daughter, knowing very well that this woman wouldn't come into my life until we both knew how to care for another unselfishly—to truly be able to love. Once I knew Kindr and I had met before our time together on earth, I then realized Tunkal and I had known one another before as well—for she had been my wolf. And I had been her friend who tried caring for her unselfishly.

I imagine this lifetime, which I just shared with you, has inspired questions. For now, please hold them and leave today's time together knowing that you are now almost ready to have your destined partner appear one night, at your campsite . . . .

February 5, 2010

Hello, dear one. You appeared unhappy this morning. However, this afternoon you're much more relaxed and clear.
What occurred to support your movement forward with
your attitude? Actually, perhaps you ought to share what
upset you, before you talk about how you passed through it.

There are multiple things I could point to that triggered my
unhappiness. This has been a challenging week, and I haven't
spoken with anyone about the incidents. I believed that it wasn't
worth expending the energy. And yet, I woke up today, here
at the end of the week, and felt like sharing the events. I see
that sometimes I need human interaction. I spend so much time
in my spirit that I didn't think talking would serve the highest
good. I was wrong.

It was snowing again today, all the businesses were closed
and I needed a break. So I called my mother. As I recited my list
of woes, there was one thing that became illuminated, and it had

to do with the manuscript. We spent the majority of the phone call speaking about it. You see, I hadn't shared the manuscript with anyone prior, which felt right. But today I did, and that felt right also. My mother was actually quite affected by the content I shared. She found the information interesting and important, and that's a lot for my Jewish skeptic mother.

Her response offered me some assurance that another human being, other than myself, would enjoy and receive benefit from this manuscript. I felt inspired enough to look past all the other challenges on my list and go back to writing.

> I'm moved at how you've been able to be so very quiet with all the recorded material you and I have created together. I'm most amazed at how no information before today has been uttered to anyone. I would now enjoy having you know more about anything you desire. My dear one, our sharing together like this will only present itself a few more times. Therefore, let us leave nothing unspoken. Know that I do intend to continue to share alone with you. And I believe that more available time will arrive in the future to converse again for the benefit of others.

I've been sensing a winding down, and it does feel like only for now. Having said that, I'd like you to talk on a topic that could benefit from some light shed on it: abortion.

> Let it be known how fully aware I am of how painful it is for anyone faced with an unwanted pregnancy to have to make a decision to either hold onto their offspring or let them return to the spirit realm. To illustrate this, I'm going to share another one of my lifetimes with you. This time, I thought I was in love. Her family didn't want her to marry

me. In their opinion, I wasn't an appropriate suitor. We let some time pass, to see if this would change. It didn't. So, we decided to leave the village that we called home. Our time together, as it turned out, ought not to have been. Not because of what her parents thought of me, but due to the challenging times that came soon after our departure.

It presented itself clearly in the beginning that we were fairly incompatible as friends, but our sexual passion for each other flamed higher than either one of us knew how to ignore. The passion didn't last long, and our friendship disappeared as well. Fortunately, our tribe believed in allowing two people who weren't happy together to end their commitment peacefully. Her parents took her home to their native land, and I left where we had lived together in order to begin anew.

Some years passed before we saw each other again. Her tribe was on their way to a new home, traveling over the land in which I was living with another woman—one who had borne my child.

I'll never forget her face, upon seeing the child. The color drained out of it, and she started to cry. I welcomed her into my home, to allow us privacy to talk. I asked how her life had become so despairing. She told me that, after we had separated, her womb filled with our child. Her mother convinced her to let the small one go back into the universe—due to its having been partly made of my blood. Her heart not only rejected the idea, it died a little each year after agreeing to her mother's "suggestion."

I, too, developed sadness—despite all the joy within my own family. My incarnation in enduring this experience became quite important in my overall journey. My heart hurts any time people allow harsh and cruel punishment to find its way toward themselves, or others, around having an abortion.

My suggestion has to do with inviting in more consciousness so that, over time, fewer and fewer unwanted pregnancies will occur. Let it be known that a significant rise in consciousness, about birth control and decision-making around one's sexual activity, would lead to a much called for decrease in unwanted pregnancies. This would therefore alter your planet's disharmony around this difficult issue.

February 8, 2010

Dear one, Mary our Mother would like to now share what one of her lifetimes showed her, in situations when a woman didn't want to have a child but was already pregnant. Are you alright with Mary coming into our conversation?

Yes, I am. I'm also surprised at your question. I have yet to stop being amazed that this is so much a part of my life.

Mary:

Hello, dear daughter. I am delighted to join you in such an important project in which I have, until now, only been a witness. Please know that my beloved daughters and sons have nothing to fear, for I will not judge anyone. My intention in sharing on this topic has only to do with a sincere desire to impart the information that, in my opinion, is crucial.

Many lifetimes ago, I felt alone in the world. I lived by myself out of town, north of the Galilee in Israel. Young women from nearby villages would come to talk with me about their lives. Some lives included boys they knew and hoped to be loved by one day, while others' were much more tragic. Many of the girls didn't know how babies were conceived, due to lack of education.

By this time, you may or may not have come to realize that my job was to facilitate in the termination of these girls' unwanted pregnancies. I also cared for them while they healed afterward. I heard many stories about why sex became a part of these people's lives so early on. There were girls who had been molested by relatives—fathers, brothers—and those who had been promised devotion in return for the fulfillment of sexual desire. Despite the reasons, and there were many, all of the young girls had one common thread connecting them. Each did not want to have a child.

I share this lifetime of mine with you now, so that you and your global brothers and sisters can know I saw enormous pain while working with these young women. However, I'm fully aware that a greater sorrow would have occurred if I had not done the work.

I know I have now brought the topic of sexual abuse into our conversation. I did this to have it be known that Jesus and I cannot command sexual abuse of children to end, despite our deep longing to do so. Nor are we capable of ending sexual violence of any kind. What we can do, however, is ask that those who feel tempted to do any act outside of their true nature (their divine nature), call on either one of us. We could then appear, to hold, to console, and to make the person aware that they are deeply treasured. For it is in forgetting this that darkness is able to cover one's own light.

Now I would appreciate any commentary from you, dear. I'm interested in your experience as a guidance counselor, back when you were in New York City working in the public schools.

I'm disturbed by what you brought forth. I'm also quite glad. This topic of child sexual abuse has not been addressed yet. And it's so important to acknowledge its presence in society. As a school counselor, I was in a most fortunate role. It was my job to build trust with children in order to become their confidant. When something wrong was going on outside of school, often I would learn of it. At that point, all the necessary people would be notified to help ensure the child's protection.

During my time in this position, there were a few sexual abuse cases. It was heart wrenching, yet also fulfilling, to be able to intervene and end it. I always let the child know that telling me was exactly the right thing for him or her to do. And I assured them that they did nothing to provoke the behavior from the perpetrator.

As I before mentioned, I experienced a few cases where sexual abuse was the issue. However, I was in this field for almost a decade and calling Child Protective Services was a regular event. I bring this into our conversation because of the amount of physical abuse, neglect, and emotional abuse to which I was privy. It's so important that people who can make a difference be aware of the prevalence. And it is so important that people who are engaging in this behavior take steps to find a way out of it!

Mary:
My dear, thank you for your sharing. If anyone hurting a child could know how he or she is not only damaging him or her self and the child, but also damaging harmony

throughout planet earth, perhaps he or she would welcome help in healing themselves—instead of continuing to injure others.

I know our time together is coming to an end for today. I want to leave you now with my heart's wish. It's for everyone to know that, despite their belief, they have each been perfectly created. Dear one, this goes for you, also. I see how you're constantly challenged by your belief that you are not acting in one hundred percent support of what is in the highest good at every moment. Please be aware of how perfect you actually are. Not believing this truth only makes you suffer. This also creates distance from your divine nature. Through this time away, darkness is given the opportunity to emerge from slumber—bringing with it all your unwanted feelings of doubt, fear, and discouragement. Let yourself remember that you are divine energy of the Creators. This will cancel out the darkness. May you always remember this.

February 9, 2010

＿＿＿＿＿

I'm filled with joy, knowing that all you and I have spoken about I regard as important. How about if today you choose the next issue in need of illumination.

What comes to mind right away is the topic of past lives. You've shared a few of yours, and have spoken of them as if they're quite matter-of-fact. However, there are people who don't believe that we've had lives other than the one we're presently living.

I know that, until a few years ago, I was on the fence about them. It was in healing school when I began to consciously experience specific past lives and became confident of their existence. What can you say about them, and their importance?

Despite any non-belief, I know how significant one's past lives are to the course of one's present lifetime.

I've been talking about some of my past lives because

I've learned many lessons from remembering them. And I believe it would be this way for all who do the same.

Time on the planet ought not be filled with so much difficulty. Discovering one's past lives is meant to be used for understanding present circumstances, and to heal from any of the past-life circumstances that cause suffering now. As you're aware, there are so many people who live alone in their discomfort; without understanding why their lives took the turns they did.

There have been a few lifetimes during which you and I have known each other as different people. During one of our lifetimes together, you were a very dear friend and we had intimate conversations. This can help you understand how our present close relationship developed.

An initial step one could take in discovering what other lives he or she may have lived, is to abstain from judgment. By withholding judgment, there's a greater possibility that one will find clarity on this matter. Secondly, taking an honest look at one's present relationships, career, and interests will offer a wealth of information. The answers lie in what brings joy as well as pain; and in what draws and what repels. Allowing for quiet meditation time to envision the possibilities is highly recommended. So is feeling into one's whole being to get a sense about what is accurate or not, and then knowing and trusting what is found.

Dear one, would you speak now about your experience with getting to know the truth about one of your past lives— and how the information is so vital to your present life?

I was thirty-five when I began having visions of myself in a teepee doing what appeared to be my work. At the time, I was on a leave of absence from the Department of Education that was about to expire. I had to decide if I was going to return to work in a position I felt was no longer suitable for me, or if I was going to resign with no immediate income prospects.

During my leave, I worked at various teaching jobs—none of which felt right. During this period, my father also died. (Actually, it was four years ago today.) I decided to take some time off and focus on doing artwork. The process felt fulfilling but when it came time to consider it my fulltime employment, it didn't feel meaningful enough. Through it all, whenever I was quiet and still, I would have the vision of myself sitting on the ground inside the teepee with people coming to visit me for something to help them feel better. This felt very familiar to me, and right for my present work. However, it also seemed highly unlikely, due to how different it was from mainstream culture.

A year went by. I had decided to resign from my position as a guidance counselor, and was open to my new calling. A serendipitous phone call then came into my life and it propelled me to energy healing school. I decided to do this to explore my sensitivity to the energy of people, places, and things—all of which I felt deeply. My intention was to go with what was true when it came to the outcome; I would either receive needed healing or I would learn to be a healer. I didn't expect both to occur, but it did.

More accurately, however, I learned healing techniques— and realized that I was already a healer. One day, early on in school, we were guided to go back to our first incarnation. It was then that I saw myself sitting on the ground of a teepee. I was biting out the poison from someone's body. I then spit it out and put my hands over the person, in a gesture of offering heal- ing energy. The scene then shifted to some people from the tribe dancing around the patient outside, while he lay on the earth. I had been a medicine woman, and finding my way to healing school brought it all back to me. The awareness of this past life has been a significant part of me being able to be fully present in this life. Every encounter since has felt important. I've been led places in order to heal other past lives. There have been people I needed to meet to heal the wounds we had experienced together before this lifetime. And I continue to do past-life healing as I sense these unresolved experiences emerge.

Thank you for the sharing you did today. My hope is for our readers to receive guidance about their past lives through their visions and intuition as well. My hope is also that those who continue to not believe will look deeply at all they already believe, revaluate, and allow room for new possibilities. I know a day will come when all the children of Creation will be clear that their ending leads to another beginning.

February 10, 2010

The wind is quite fierce today. I can feel her spirit needing its freedom of expression; like mine last night. You encouraged me to dance. I resisted your proposal. I was tired. You were persistent. I'm glad you were. My spirit tasted the movement it needed. I also felt your loving energy surrounding me. Thank you.

I enjoyed last night's dance also! And I know that statement doesn't make for the typical smooth transition into today's topic. And yet . . . I so often hear people wanting to know what will happen to them once they die. Today's joy is in being able to offer this information. When a human dies from natural causes (which means it was their destined time), their body remains earthbound and their soul moves through the atmosphere into a place that is surrounded by only white light. No one meets them there. However, later on, once they have let go of all their earthly energy, angelic beings take them to another place in which interaction can occur if a soul identifies another soul it knows. For previously departed family may or may not have already reincarnated. Many souls do, however, remain in this place for quite some time before reincarnating. Despite what most people have heard, there is no one who physically looks as they did when they lived on the earth. So, what allows for the identification is energy sensitivity. Every soul's energy field is uniquely their own. Another aspect of death has to do with finding out why one lived; finding out one's soul's purpose. For some, this comes as no surprise—but for most, it's an opportunity to relearn it.

Reality is clearly known in this sphere. For the truth is solely acknowledged. My fellow angels share all that is needed to be known, so that each soul can be with one another with absolutely no blame for the experience of any earthly pain. The souls can then enjoy one another as well as honoring each other's journey. Only souls who have allowed their destined death to occur without intervening are welcomed here.

There is a different place for souls who take their own life. Not only is it farther away from earth, it's darker. No one leaves there until they become clear about why they intervened, and disrupted not only their destined path but also the paths of the close friends and family they left behind. When clarity comes through quiet solitude, the before-mentioned place becomes available to them. Self-forgiveness is of paramount importance in order to move on.

The last group of souls I'm going to discuss are those who are victims of someone else's crime that results in an un-destined death. Both victim and perpetrator go to a holding place where angelic beings run and facilitate reconciliation exercises, in order to encourage peace between the two sides. Once this is achieved, they then move to the place where all souls are equal, relaxed, and planning their next incarnation.

The hope of the Creators is that all souls will fulfill their destinies without interruption. My wish is that all people would enjoy their lives more than they currently do—despite the fact that one has the opportunity to live another life, it's always the present one that matters most! Everything one can do to be fully present for it ought to be done. Let it be known how significant it is to slow down and to feel each and every moment's breath.

This is quite the inside scoop you've shared—once again. It all sounds rather peaceful. Yet, I hope I don't experience it for a long time to come. Does it help if you know someone?!

Listening to you inspired a question. What's the difference between spirit and soul? I sense a difference, but I'd like you to make it clearer.

Of course. One's spirit includes the body and the mind and one's soul includes one's spirit. You don't need to understand any more than this. Clarity about this comes from experiencing the truth for one's self—not by thinking about it and trying to make it into rational sense.

One knows when he or she is approaching life through the spirit or the soul. Subtle but vital changes occur. Life is more peaceful when it's lived from the soul. A cause or a mission becomes free of its anticipated perils or gains. Relationships of all types lose their attachments to the outcomes of circumstances. And love is truly known all the time, due to the clarity of understanding the connected-ness of all things.

I wish I'd asked about this sooner. However, I believe I needed to hear you speak on the various topics to have the clarity to ask this question. I feel I've overlooked this difference, perhaps for too long.

I want to assure you that you haven't. It's perfect timing. Whenever one is ready for something, an opportunity arises for it to be accepted or be put off for another time. As long as the opportunity to develop more awareness is welcomed at some point, rather than it being continually avoided, the timing remains perfect.

February 12, 2010

I'm here with you today, our last day, to let it be known how appreciative I am for all the time you spent with me in order to share the information that we have. My hope is that those who want to hear what we've shared will have access to the material. And that anyone ready for his or her evolution will not be afraid of what might be left behind, after any necessary letting-go has taken place. I encourage allowing all that doesn't support one's journey to fall away, while remaining peaceful with the knowledge that only the most highly supportive circumstances will then beckon them home.

I want all the Creators' daughters and sons to not fear what is unknown, what is not immediately understood, and what is unable to be seen in a conventional manner. Now is the time to let one's truth be heard and actualized. Settling for anything other than that is what ought to be feared.

I will now offer time for you to bring up anything you yet wish to understand. For I feel a completeness in all I intended to share.

Thank you for the last words of wisdom. And thank you for including me in all this sacred text. Although it's not something I anticipated happening, it does makes sense as I look back over the growing you intimately assisted me with, over the past few years. I reckon I was being honed . . . .

There are more questions and topics, but I know this is enough for now . . . so I'm going to end with letting you know how appreciative I also am for all the time you shared with me! And I look forward to dancing again with you when the time is right, both on the page and on the floor . . . .

Peace and much love for you, soul brother.

To be continued . . .

Subject Index

About the Author

Alexis Eldridge is an artist, a healer, and is devoted to her spiritual path, which has become her entire way of life.

She was born and raised in New York, where she also attended both Hunter and Brooklyn College, CUNY. She earned a Bachelor of Arts in Psychology and a Master of Science in Education. She stayed in New York City upon graduation and worked as a public school guidance counselor, seeing special education children in a clinical setting.

Alexis felt called to explore other work in her early thirties. Without knowing what that was, she resigned, travelled, created, and ultimately found her way to energy healing school. She then moved to Virginia, where she established a healing practice and wrote this book.

She is excited about what's showing up on her journey—now that she's been showing up for *it* more fully . . . .

Rainbow Ridge Books publishes spiritual
and metaphysical titles, and is distributed by Square
One Publishers in Garden City Park, New York.

To contact authors and editors, peruse our titles, and
see submission guidelines, please visit our website at:

www.rainbowridgebooks.com.

For orders and catalogs, please call toll-free:
(877) 900-BOOK.